THE COMPLETE
WEST HIGHLAND WHITE TERRIER

The Complete
WEST HIGHLAND
WHITE TERRIER

By John T. Marvin

Fourth Edition
Fifth Printing—1983

HOWELL BOOK HOUSE INC.

230 PARK AVENUE
NEW YORK, N.Y.   10169

Also by John T. Marvin:
THE COMPLETE CAIRN TERRIER
THE COMPLETE SCOTTISH TERRIER
THE BOOK OF ALL TERRIERS

"The Watchers." Currier and Ives print, pre 1872.

Copyright © 1977, 1971, 1965, 1961 by Howell Book House Inc.

Library of Congress Catalog Card No. 76–58225

ISBN 0-87605-355-X

Printed in U.S.A.

To my wife,
whose initial interest in
the Westie led me to become
devoted to the breed.

"Cave Canem"—Beware of the Dog.
Mosaic found in Pompeii.

Contents

"The Breakfast Party," circa 1831, by Sir Edwin Landseer. This painting was also exhibited under the title "Too Hot." It shows early highland terriers of various types with a hound.

Foreword to the Fourth Edition

Shortly after the first edition of *The Complete West Highland White Terrier* was published, the legendary Ch. Elfinbrook Simon was named Best in Show at Westminster. Since then the fortunes of "Colonel Malcolm's favorite" have soared beyond all expectations.

Since Simon's great win, the Westie has achieved unprecedented general acclaim across the United States and Canada. During the same period *The Complete West Highland White Terrier* has achieved the deserved status of a classic. It now goes into its fourth great edition—an edition that makes the Westie's story current. Here are the dogs and fanciers, past and present, that have earned for the breed the fame it enjoys today. Here also are the practical considerations of keeping, showing, breeding and enjoying these delightful dogs to the utmost.

The Complete West Highland White Terrier has always enjoyed the endorsement of the fancy. This is so, in part, because it happens to be a fine book for novice and veteran alike. The other reason for the book's great acclaim is its author.

In the Westie fancy John Marvin's name is a household word. He has been active in dogs for over 40 years. With Mrs. Marvin, he has bred and shown some of the breed's finest under the Cranbourne prefix. He has been licensed to judge all terriers since 1947 and is consistently in demand as a judge whose opinions carry weight. His judging credits are impressive and include the WHWTCA national Specialty, Westminster and numerous other prestige shows.

For many years his activities have been a benefit to the entire dog game. From 1951 to 1955 he was President of the Ohio Dog Owners' Association and is currently serving on the Eastern Trial Board of the American Kennel Club. He is the AKC Delegate for the West Highland White Terrier Club of America and a past President of the WHWTCA and the American Fox Terrier Club.

Many are familiar with Mr. Marvin's scholarly contributions to various dog journals. He has written regularly for *Pure-bred Dogs—American Kennel Gazette, Showdogs* and many other highly respected periodicals. His *Jottings and Trimmings* column in the Parent Club *Bulletin* is avidly read by all members of the WHWTCA. His writings have earned him many awards including Dog Writer of the Year for 1973. He was elected President of the Dog Writers' Association of America in 1973 and continues in that office at the present time.

Preparing the fourth edition of this great classic has been a particular pleasure for me. As a professional editor, it is a joy to work with one as qualified as the author, and as an active fancier of the West Highland it is a privilege to be involved with the "Marvin" book from the ground up. I wholeheartedly recommend this new edition to all my fellow Westie fans in the knowledge that you will enjoy reading it as much as I have enjoyed preparing it.

—SEYMOUR N. WEISS
Editor and
WHWTCA Columnist
Pure-bred Dogs—American Kennel Gazette

Preface

The purpose of this book is to give the West Highland White Terrier owner a complete and accurate source of information concerning the breed, its background and its characteristics. Since the publication of the first edition, constant and never-ending research—in which I have been aided in many instances by friends of the breed—has uncovered considerable additional historical material. All of the many important facts brought to light have been incorporated into this fourth edition, with aim to make it as complete and accurate as possible.

In addition, much has happened since the first publication of this book in 1961. The breed has matured and grown beyond even the expectations of its most enthusiastic supporters. Today, the Highlander is one of the top Terrier breeds, both in this country and in England. The challenge offered by this preferred position has been enthusiastically accepted by breed fanciers the world over, and the Westie has become one of the most highly respected in Terrier group and all-breed competition. The developments over the past few years dictate an entire change of perspective on the breed, and this present effort has been revised, re-worded and enlarged to reflect this condition.

In order to make the book more easily understood, I have used as many illustrations as possible and have included a host of historical pictures to aid in the delineation of the breed's development. Many of these are offered for the first time in this edition, and add great interest to the more or less obscure early beginnings of our breed. Of course, current winners have been used to bring the pictorial history up-to-date. In addition, there are many drawings to illustrate points of information that are difficult to explain and/or understand. Of prime importance is the newly offered trimming section, illustrated by a series of artist's drawings prepared by Clarence C. Fawcett, himself a Westie enthusiast. These drawings were made as the author actually trimmed a Highlander, and demonstrate pictorially, proper step-by-step trimming techniques. My sincere thanks to Mr. Fawcett for his permission to use these drawings, as well as for his efforts.

Appreciation is also expressed to my wife for her help and patience throughout the work entailed in writing the book and its several revisions. I also wish to thank the many friends and Westie owners, in America, Canada and England, who have generously supplied information and photographs for the book, for without their help the task would have been impossible. I specifically want to mention the tremendous aid given me by the late Mrs. C. C. Pacey in the initial delineation of the British aspects of the work. Mrs. Pacey helped me immeasurably with information and photos, many of which have great historical import. I also appreciate the assistance given me by members of the staff of the American Kennel Club and of the Kennel Club in England. Their prompt responses to my many questions on the breed helped tremendously.

As this book goes into its fourth edition, every effort has been made to make all of its material current. Statistics, listings, and other data have been revised, and several items of information have been corrected, to reflect the more detailed and accurate particulars that have been obtained. The several chapters concerning show ring activities have been up-dated to include current winners and events as well as continuing to record past memorable moments.

It is hoped sincerely that each of you will enjoy reading this book as much as I have writing it.

JOHN T. MARVIN

Step Brothers

The special appeal of Westie puppies hasn't changed much in the past sixty-plus years as illustrated by "The Step Brothers" from a painting by G. T. Leibgan, circa 1914. From the author's collection.

"Puffin Shooting." Lithograph after T. M. Baynes, circa 1830. This very rare print of an unusual sport includes typical highland dogs of the period. These ranged in color from black to white and were selected for on the basis of working quality alone.

A group of terriers of the 1860s including three of Scottish heritage. The dog at the extreme left is probably an early Cairn. A Westie is seen in the left foreground facing a dog of Dandie Dinmont stamp. The others are a Manchester, a Fox Terrier and a Bull Terrier.

The Background of the Westie

Volumes have been written concerning the dog, its origin and habits. This book, while being directed primarily to the West Highland White Terrier, will attempt to provide a useful working background for the novice while serving to refresh the memories of more serious fanciers in matters of general interest.

The basic genealogy of the dog is completely obscured in the dimness of the past. Undoubtedly, all breeds of dog descended from common ancestors and these same ancestors were probably those of the wolf.* The osteology of the wolf is similar to that of the dog, and the wolf and dog cohabit freely, lending credence to the claim of descent from the same progenitors.

The Shepherd's dog is sometimes credited as the dog most nearly approaching the primitive race and the dog from which the Terrier descended through the Hound, as set forth in the Genealogical Table of Buffon.† In his book, *Rural Sports*, Daniel agrees that cohabitation between the wolf and the dog does occur and that hybrids of varying degrees of ferocity are produced, as evidenced by the early Siberian dogs. He doubts,

* *Youatt On The Dog*, 1845
† *Rural Sports*, by Daniel, 1802

15

however, that any wolf blood flows in the veins of the truly domesticated dog.

Regardless of its origin, the dog has been known to man for as long as records have been kept. The Bible refers to them more than forty times in the Old and New Testaments.* Figures of dogs and dog-like deities have been found carved in relief on ancient works of stone, the earliest being on the Tomb of Amten in Egypt, which dates back to the Fourth Dynasty, or between 3500 and 4000 B.C. Appreciation of a dog's fidelity led the early Egyptians to apply the designation of "Dog Star" to Sirius. This, the brightest star in the heavens, always appeared as a forerunner to the periodic floods of the river Nile, and was a signal for the shepherds to move their flocks to higher ground. Its appearance was so reliable that these simple people believed it to be a symbol of watchfulness and fidelity and, hence, named it after the dog, who was always held in great veneration by the ancient tribes of the Pharaohs. In old Roman dwellings, a chained dog was often depicted on the mosaic threshold with the accompanying words *Cave Canem* (beware of the dog). The early Europeans used the dog as a symbol of fidelity and loyalty. Ecclesiastical representations of holy patrons are replete with dogs; Saint Benignus has a dog by his side; Saint Bernard is shown with a dog at his feet; and Saint Sira is pictured with dogs about her. From earliest history, dogs have been the protectors of the habitation of man. In every age and in all parts of the globe, dogs have played an important part in the labors and sports of men, sharing trial, danger, and pleasure with equal zeal.

> The poor dog in life, the firmest friend,
> The first to welcome, foremost to defend:
> Whose honest heart is still his master's own,
> Who labours, fights, lives, breathes for him alone.
>   —Byron

Throughout centuries of civilization, canines have been the true and constant friends of the human race. They have full

* *The Complete Dog Book*, 1975.

and unqualified respect for persons of all creeds, races, and stations of life, asking only a little praise and affection in payment for their unfailing devotion. In short, the steadfastness and fidelity of the dog is unmatched by any other member of the animal world.

> With eye upraised, his master's looks to scan,
> The joy of solace, and the aid of man;
> The rich man's guardian, and the poor man's friend,
> The only creature, faithful to the end.
>
> —Crabbe

Other domesticated animals submit to human control but rarely do they recognize their master except in connection with the supplying of their wants. A dog, on the other hand, will starve with its master and suffer any hardship or indignity in order to be close to the object of its affection. Many dogs have been known to grieve over the loss of their masters to the extent of refusing food and drink and finally dying of broken hearts—where can one find greater love?

Early concepts of the utilitarian advantages of the dog varied little from today's views. Dogs have been used as drovers, dray animals, hunters, vermin destroyers, and companions. Today, their use differs not at all; we probably stress their companionship to a greater degree, but the canine still has the same definite uses to which ends it exerts its every effort. The advent of police, guard, and guide work has even extended the field of purposeful existence that has always been that of man's best friend.

To obtain a better insight into the canine race, the zoological ranking and biological background of the animal will be of interest. The dog belongs to that division of quadrupeds termed *vertebrata,* and it ranks in the class *mammalia* because the female suckles her young. It is of the tribe *unguiculata,* since it is armed with nails or claws which are not retractile, and is of the order of *digitigrades* because it walks on its toes. The dog is of the genus *canis,* in view of its tooth arrangement, and belongs to the sub-genus *familiaris* by reason of the round shape of the

17

pupil of its eye, which distinguishes it from the wolf, fox, and jackal, all of which stem from the same genus.

Members of the genus *canis* are basically carnivorous animals; that is, they are primarily meat eaters. The dog is equipped for such a diet with an excellent set of forty-two teeth, including twelve incisors (small front teeth) that are adapted for cutting and seizing; four canines (the long pointed tusk-like dentition) which are for tearing, stabbing, or for "fixing" the struggling prey; and twenty-six premolars and molars (the broader, heavy rear teeth having substantially flat complex crowns) that are used as grinders for crushing food. The milk dentition, or first teeth (puppy teeth), are fewer in number, since certain of the molars and premolars have no predecessors. In general, the permanent teeth begin to replace the puppy teeth at about four months of age.

The dog tears its food and often bolts large pieces with little or no mastication. The stomach is of simple structure capable of digesting this unchewed food, and the intestines are of length medium between the short ones of the true *carnivora* and the long ones of *graminivorous* animals. For these reasons, dogs can easily digest divers foods, including grains and vegetables in addition to meat and, therefore, thrive on mixed diets.

From the beginning of the recorded history of the dog, different breeds or strains have been known. Dogs have for centuries been selectively bred by man for the purpose at hand. As the need for a different type arose, that type was bred. Bird dogs, sight and scent Hounds, workers, fighters, and Terriers are but a few of the many special types that have been bred.

Since dogs are tractable and easily trained for almost any purpose, it has been a relatively easy task to modify and change characteristics of a breed or variety and by selection and cross-breeding to obtain the type of animal desired. This statement is readily proved by the fact that in 1873 only forty breeds and varieties were known, whereas today some 300 breeds and varieties are recognized throughout the world.

All modern breeds of dogs are hybrids—crosses of various breeds and strains to obtain the desired characteristics. When these crosses, through selection and several generations of reproduction, breed true, the characteristics of the breed may be termed "set" and a new breed is established. Today's 122 recognized distinct breeds (1977) of dogs have all attained this station. They are "set" in their characteristics and conformation. Occasional throwbacks occur, but the great majority of their progeny breed reasonably true to type.

The British Isles was the birthplace of that grouping of dogs known as "Terriers" and in this family of canines belongs our West Highland White. Terriers, as evidenced by their Group name (derived from the Latin, "Terra," meaning earth), are earth dogs, dogs that go to ground for their prey. They are of special temperament, have high intelligence and unquestioned courage. They will fight to the death rather than yield ground or give quarter. And, above all, they respect man.

An interesting description of a "Terrier" was written in 1774 by Oliver Goldsmith, who said: "The terrier is a small kind of hound, with rough hair, made use of to force the fox and badger out of their holes; or rather to give notice by their barking, in what part of their kennel the fox or badger resides, when the sportsmen intend to dig them out."

This description calls for the Terrier to be a barking dog, one bred not only to fight the fox and badger, etc., but also "to give notice" where they reside. Thus, the Terrier, when he went to ground, was expected to bark constantly to tell the hunter where he was going so that the earth could be dug and the prize captured and killed. Sportsmen for many years have had little care for a Terrier without "good voice," and one who is so deficient is no Terrier at all. For these reasons, we can expect today's Terrier to enjoy a lusty bark when conditions demand; it is his heritage.

A very early reference* suggests that a good breed of "Terrier" comes from "a Beagle and a mongrel Mastiff, or from

* *Rural Sports*, by Daniel, 1802

19

any small thick-skinned dog that had courage . . ." These Terriers presumably did not have good voice, and a "collar of bells" was placed around their necks to give notice of direction and to cause the fox to leave his den. This reference is interesting but is not in agreement with opinions of many other authorities who seemingly concur on the antiquity and qualities of the Terrier.

Reference to the forebears of the Terrier clan are found repeatedly in early treatises on dogs. Brown was the first to name the varieties of the tribe in his *Biographical Sketches and Authentic Anecdotes of Dogs,* 1829, to wit: "There are two kinds of terriers—the rough-haired Scotch and the smooth English. The Scotch is certainly the purest in point of breed and the English seems to have been produced by a cross from him. The Scotch terrier is generally low in stature, seldom more than twelve or fourteen inches in height with a strong muscular body and short stout legs; his ears small, and half-pricked; his head rather large in proportion to the size of his body, and the muzzle considerably pointed; his scent is extremely acute, so that he can trace the footsteps of all animals with certainty; he is generally of a sandy color or black. Dogs of these colors are certainly the most hardy, and more to be depended upon; when white or pied, it is a sure mark of impurity of the breed. The hair of the terrier is long and matted and hard over almost every part of his body. His bite is extremely keen. There are three distinct varieties of the Scotch terrier, viz: The one above described. Another, about the same size and form, but with hair much longer and somewhat flowing, which gives his legs the appearance of being very short. This is the prevailing breed of the Western Islands of Scotland. The third variety is much larger, etc."

This description does well for the West Highlander except for the comment on color. Other authors have not been so harsh when whites appeared in the litter. In fact, Sydenham Edwards, in his *Cynographia Britannica,* published in 1800, expounds at length on the Terrier but gives an entirely different

Scotch Terriers (1835, by Smith)

"Waiting" or sometimes called "Highland Dogs," circa 1839 by Landseer; showing a Highland Terrier in the foreground.

view on color. "The terrier—so-called from earthing or entering holes after its game . . ." comes in several varieties, "The most distinct varieties are the crooked-legged and the straight-legged; their colours generally black with tanned leggs and muzzle, a spot of the same colour over each eye; though they are sometimes reddish-fallow or white and pied. The white kind have been in request of late years."

Further substantiation of the existence and desirability of white dogs is offered by Thomas Bell, who wrote in his *History of British Quadrupeds* (1837) that the "Scottish kind of Terrier" had rough harsh hair and was "generally dirty white" in color, although he agrees with others that there was a wide variation in color among members of the variety. C. L. Martin corroborated this observation some eight years later when he wrote in his *History of the Dog* (1845) that the Scotch variety of Terrier was short of limb and had a wire-haired coat "of a white or sandy color".

The great authority, Rawdon Lee, writing in *Modern Dogs* (1894) upheld the antiquity of the Scotch branch of the Terrier tribe, stating: "From what I have been told and from what I have read, I believe that this little dog (Scotch Terrier) is the oldest variety of the canine race indigenous to north Britain, although a comparatively recent introduction across the border and into fashionable society—at any rate under his present name."

These early Scotch Terriers were referred to in literature by many names which today are directed to separate and distinct breeds. This has led to much confusion. However, study of many reference books and old dog prints shows that Terriers of different appearance, size, and shape all carried the same name at one time or another. This fact gives basis for the thought that many of the present day Scotch breeds of Terriers have been existent for many years, albeit in various states of refinement and development.

The exact origin of the basic Terrier blood is so obscure that it discourages conjecture. Early writers on dogs refer to any earth dog as a Terrier, as noted above, and German scientists have written for many years of short-legged, generally long-backed dogs under the generic term "Basset." This grouping has included Dachshunds, Basset Hounds and "Terriers." The basis for this grouping and its true interpretation are not known, although the general outline of the breeds in question lends some right to the belief that all of these short-legged breeds were derived from common basic blood.

The development of the distinct breeds and strains known today was the result of purposeful breeding techniques practiced by early breeders who carefully chose the parents and selected only the best of the "get" for reproductive purposes. The young dogs were trained for their work and the most adept and biddable were again bred, with careful selection, to assure courage and determination. As time progressed, crosses with other breeds were introduced to yield special characteristics indigenous to those breeds. Among the Terriers, the Hound was used to increase keenness of scent and improve disposition. Crosses with fighting dog breeds were introduced to intensify tenacity and increase courage. In fact, the several Terrier breeds include many infusions which yielded for their wise breeders the types of dogs desired.

As their name implies, Terriers were originally bred to destroy ground animals, and, for this pursuit, they are still adept. They kill rats, foxes, otters, badgers, and all other vermin that have the temerity to cross their path. Larger breeds of Terriers will fight it out with anything on four legs, and the Airedale has been used successfully to hunt mountain lion and bear.*

As time went on, different sections of the country, different towns, and even different large estates developed distinct strains of the more basic Terrier breeds which best suited their limited purpose. From these strains come our present day Terrier breeds.

* *All About Airedales,* R. M. Palmer, 1911

A listing of the related dogs in the Terrier Group (Group IV) as recognized by the American Kennel Club (1977) is as follows:

Airedale Terrier
American Staffordshire Terrier
Australian Terrier
Bedlington Terrier
Border Terrier
Bull Terrier (White)
Bull Terrier (Colored)
Cairn Terrier
Dandie Dinmont Terrier
Fox Terrier (Wire)
Fox Terrier (Smooth)
Irish Terrier
Kerry Blue Terrier
Lakeland Terrier
Manchester Terrier
Norwich Terrier
Schnauzer (Miniature)
Scottish Terrier
Sealyham Terrier
Skye Terrier
Soft-Coated Wheaten Terrier
Staffordshire Bull Terrier
Welsh Terrier
West Highland White Terrier

All members of the Terrier family have the instinctive desire to enjoy a good frolic or a fight. This should not be taken as a condemnation that all Terriers are fighters; they are not, and this is particularly true of the West Highlander. However, no Terrier has ever been known to back away from a fight or act the coward—it is just not breed character. In fact, the courage indigenous to all Terrier breeds can best be traced to early training and environment. It has been retold many times

24

that "keepers" of kennels for the Scotch gentry would test the young dogs for gameness before they decided to add them to the working pack. This test frequently consisted of dropping the dog into an upended barrel in which a young badger, or other equally ferocious foe, was waiting. If the dog killed or mortally wounded his adversary, he was considered a worthy addition to the pack. If not, few tears were shed.

This method of determining gameness seems "extreme" today, but it was a realistic approach in the days when the main purpose of the Terrier was to rout out or kill the game in its earth. It is also the reason why today's Terriers are so fearless, for with the test outlined above, few that were not game survived to father descendants.

In spite of this early training, Terriers are proud, friendly, affectionate, and intelligent. They make wonderful pets and companions, and few who have ever owned a Terrier will consider any other breed as a replacement when that sad need arises in their lives.

Two highland terriers rabbiting are the subjects of this painting by P. Jones (1858). Colors varied in the mid-19th Century and ear cropping was not uncommon. *Courtesy of Gerald Massey.*

Colonel Malcolm with some of his Westies in the early 1900s.

West Highland White Terriers at the Inverailort Kennels of Mrs. Cameron-Head, about 1909.

The West Highland White Terrier

The basic Terrier background is the heritage of the West Highland White. The "Westie" or "Highlander," as he is sometimes called, is a smallish dog stemming from the basic Scotch branch of the Terrier family. He has great agility and is quick in movement with tremendous stamina and courage unsurpassed by any member of the Terrier clan. The Westie needed these attributes in his native Scotland, where rocks and crags and generally rough terrain made ease and quickness of movement vital if the dog was to survive the onslaughts of the foe in subterranean battle. A small Terrier could maneuver easily under difficult conditions and thus outlast his prey.

The background of many of the more recently recognized breeds of dogs is relatively easy to trace. The progenitors, selective breeding programs, and crosses with other breeds and strains to obtain desired characteristics have been more or less accurately chronicled by interested persons, making a breed history which is of a rather exact nature.

The older breeds of dog are not so fortunate. The precise background is obscure and their right to antiquity is frequently

based on a thousand and one unproven claims of their enthusiastic, if not too truthful or accurate, historians. Early history of
the Westie is based upon little written data before the remarks
made by Captain Mackie as published in Gray's *Dogs of Scotland*
(1891) * and reprinted in Davies' The Scottish Terrier (1906).
Here we find mention of Poltalloch Terriers as dogs of a "linty
white" color and weighing from 16 to 20 pounds. Mackie
describes the head as "very long" and the nose "often flesh-
coloured." He suggests that the ears are often "cream in an
otherwise white dog and the skin of the body is generally
pigmented." Mackie also took notice of a "dorsal line of cream
or fawn" in many of the specimens that he viewed. These
observations, made from actual inspection of Col. Malcolm's
early dogs, bear special attention since with the exception of the
"long heads" and the "flesh coloured noses" most are still valid
today in varying degrees. The exact dates of Mackie's visits to
Poltalloch are not documented, but undoubtedly go back quite a
way since Sir Ian Malcolm stated many years ago (but subsequent to the date of Mackie's writings) that the strain was
known and propagated at the family's Argyllshire estate for
more than one hundred years. That many of the ancestors
of today's Westie were not immaculately white is an acknowl-
edged fact—in fact many were not even white!

Col. Malcolm was known to have favored whites because of
an unfortunate hunting accident which occurred sometime
around 1860. According to the story, the Colonel was out hunting hare with one of his favorite Terriers, a reddish brown
fellow. The dog while running through the cover was mistaken
for the hare and was shot and killed. This grieved the good
Colonel, who then and there declared that he would prop-
agate only the whites in his kennel and thus avoid similar
unhappy experiences. In order to accomplish this end, he
instructed that his breeding stock be limited to "white" dogs.
Color was not bred out in a few short years—it required many
years of work. That Malcolm's Terriers were not "the useless
show-bench" type is emphasized in L. C. R. Cameron's book,
Otters and Otter Hunting, London, 1908, in which the author
refers to the white dogs as follows:

Colonel Malcolm of Poltalloch has a kennel of these ter-

---

* A one-page chapter on the Poltalloch Terrier, page 51.

riers, that his family has bred for generations, and to which he recently applied the name of West Highland White Terriers. I believe they were originally employed for the purpose of killing Otters.

This passage points to the varied purposes to which the breed was put and never found to be wanting as an avid hunter.

As late as 1910, a prominent West Highland breeder, Mrs. Cameron-Head of the Inverailort Kennels, referred to the representatives of the breed as "White and Lemon" Terriers,* indicating considerable color. And early visitors to Poltalloch described the dogs as being of a "linty white" color. Even today, off-white coats, wheaten dorsal streaks, and yellowish tinges are not uncommon.

West Highland White activity was not confined to the Malcolm family if numerous claims are to be given credence. "Earth dogges" out of Argyllshire had wide repute as early as the sixteenth century. The story is told that King James I of England was so impressed with the prowess of this strain that he made a present to a friend in France of some of the "Earth dogges out of Argyllshire." The tale does not state whether or not the dogs were of a white color, but many West Highland White enthusiasts insist that these same "dogges" were Westies.

Dr. Flaxman of Fifeshire is sometimes credited with a part in the early development of the breed.† The Malcolms decried this claim, however, and the two were great rivals in the early ring days of the breed. This is demonstrated by the unquestioned pleasure reflected in a telegram sent to the Colonel by his head keeper after a successful exhibition of the Poltalloch Terriers at an early Edinburgh show. The wire is typical of Scotch brevity and said: "We've knockit the stour oot o' Flaxman."

Another interesting, useful referrence to Flaxman is found in Lane's book, *Dog Shows and Doggy People,* 1902, pp. 100–102. Lane had great respect for Flaxman who, he says, had a Scottish Terrier bitch that kept whelping white puppies in every litter.

At first, he drowned the "sports" but then decided to breed

* *The Kennel Encyclopedia,* by Sidney Turner, 1911
† *The Scottish Terrier and West Highland White Terrier,* by McCandlish and Powlett, 1909

"Dignity and Impudence," by Sir Edwin Henry Landseer (1839).

only for whites. After ten years, he produced a strain of "White Scottish Terriers" with good pigmentation. Lane fails to even mention Malcolm and states that Flaxman devoted more time and trouble developing a variety of a popular breed than any other man living, quite a different view from most.

It is also said that George Clarke, at various times head keeper at numerous Scottish estates, brought Terriers from Mull to Inverary and thence to Roseneath, seat of the Duke of Argyll. Here they were bred with care and crossed with local Terriers to produce a very desirable strain called "Roseneath" Terriers. Since the names Poltalloch Terrier and Roseneath Terrier were used interchangeably about 1900, it is reasonable to assume that the dogs were of similar appearance; such assumption is proved to be the rule by numerous observers who state that both Terriers were one and the same breed. These names were superseded by the present nomenclature, which is said to have been fostered by Colonel Malcolm, and popularized in an effort to bring about a better feeling among breeders of the dog. The name is a good one, indicative of the native habitat of the breed—the rugged West Highlands of Scotland.

Sir Edwin Henry Landseer, noted English animal artist (1802–1873), depicted, in several early works, white dogs closely resembling the West Highland White. For example, in the painting "Dignity and Impudence" (1839) there is shown an excellent head study of what appears to be a West Highlander. Furthermore, it is a recorded fact that Landseer loved the West Highlands of Scotland and visited there many times, which would have brought him in contact with members of the breed in their native habitat. Claims are made that these paintings and facts are proof of the early origin of the Highlander. Such claims have considerable merit, since Landseer was an artist of great ability, and any portrayal by him should be a correct and faithful presentation of the subject.

Another painting by Gourlay Steell (see page 33) is of interest in this connection. The painting "Dandie Dinmont and His Terriers" was done in 1865 and shows two dogs that may be Dandies and two smaller ones that more nearly resemble Cairns or Westies. These latter two dogs are too small to be Dandies and bear no resemblance to that breed. According to Mr. Steell, "the little dog" was one of his own and therefore should be a true representation. A third definitive painting, *The Warrener's Pony, Terrier and Puppy,* dated 1876 and painted by John Emms, depicts a white Highland Terrier with her puppy, see page 33. These three early paintings strengthen further the claim that the West Highland White was rather well defined by about the middle of the nineteenth century.

Dogs of Westie type were also alleged to have been seen on the Isle of Skye and in Ross-Shire more than a century ago, but such statements lack proof. Suffice it to say that Colonel Malcolm and his family never laid claim to being the originators of the breed, although the most authentic records place this honor with the residents of Poltalloch.

There are still other theories, based on the laws of breeding, which point to the antiquity of the Highlander. It is held that throwbacks in color which occur in both the Scottish Terrier and in the Cairn stamp them as the offspring of the Westie. White patches or lockets on the chests of Scottish Terriers, a fault difficult to breed out and one so prevalent as to be permitted in moderation by the breed Standard, lend credence to a white ancestor. White paws and chest markings as well as white patches under the tail in Cairns also point to a white forebear. In the case of the Cairn, however, it is common knowledge that these breeds were interbred to a considerable extent; thus, this particular characteristic does not yield "first birth" to the Westie over the Cairn. It is probable that the Westie and Cairn, which resemble one another closely except for color, were one and the same breed, and that by color selection the strains were finally separated and bred true. This supposition seems to be substantiated by the Malcolm story of mistaking one of his dogs for a rabbit. This hypothesis is also fostered by Kate L. Stephens in her treatise on the Cairn.* Interbreeding of the Westie and the Cairn also explains the off-white coats and wheaten dorsal streaks seen today in certain strains of the Highlander.

The famous Harviestoun line of Cairn Terriers is said to owe its great success in the ring to West Highland sires.† In fact, the

* *The Scottish Terrier,* by Dorothy Gabriel
† *The Popular Cairn Terrier,* by J. W. H. Beynon

Dandie Dinmont and His Terriers by Courlay Steell, 1865. Depicts three white and one colored Terrier of the Westie stamp.

"The Warrener's Pony and Terrier and Puppy," by John Emms (1876). From the author's collection.

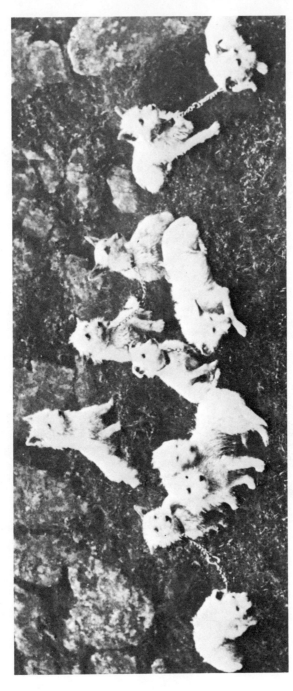

A Scottish Eleven. West Highland workers circa 1905. Note four couples chained together—also, the variation in types of ears.

pedigree of Harviestoun Raider, one of the all-time greats of the Cairn, includes a large number of West Highlanders; for example, Glenmhor Chief, Ch. Glenmhor Pride, Atholl, Inverness Wasp, Ch. Morven, and Ross-Shire Helvellyn are a few of the whites that appear.

The situation becomes more complex and interesting when some early Westie pedigrees are studied. In one 1907 pedigree of a West Highland White, the names of Callum Dhu and Seafield Rascal appear. Both are widely known Scottish Terriers and are found frequently in the extended pedigrees of present day Scottish Terriers. This same pedigree is also known to have been the exact lineage of a Cairn, Inverness Sporran. This very confusion in the extended pedigrees of early dogs of several Terrier breeds only proves more strongly that the early Scotch Terrier breeds came from common blood and frequently were found in the same litter. To relate the words of an old English judge, "In the early 1900's, all three often came from the same litter . . . according to what the buyer wanted."

Interbreeding of the Cairn and the Westie continued unabated until about 1917 when The American Kennel Club decreed that no Cairn could gain registration if its pedigree carried a West Highland White ancestor within the first three generations. This drastic though commendable action led to a similar edict by the English Kennel Club, and, thus, interbreeding was definitely stopped, although its effects are noted years later.*

The description of the old Scotch Terrier as found in Youatt † follows closely the present day West Highland White Terrier, except in color, which varied according to preference. The early Scotch Terrier was generally higher on the leg and smaller than today's Scottish Terrier and quite close in size to the Westie. He had a relatively short, thick head and varied in color from black to white, with wheatens, and pied and light colors being quite common. Whether the Westie is the original offspring of this basic Scotch Terrier, it is impossible to say. It is,

* *The Complete Cairn Terrier,* by John T. Marvin, pages 50–54.
† *Youatt on the Dog,* 1845

however, undoubtedly true that the West Highland White, Scottish, Cairn, Dandie Dinmont, and Skye Terriers all came from this same source and that all were in the process of breed development during contemporaneous periods of time. Such an explanation seems most plausible, since it instantly explains many factors in the backgrounds of these several breeds that heretofore were difficult to reconcile when studying them as separate and distinct strains of varying antiquity.

During the period of from about 1880 to 1900 there was a tendency to elongate the heads of all breeds emanating from the basic blood, and the illustration (on page 38) of a Scottish Terrier and a West Highlander side by side clearly shows the success of the venture. (Note also the coloration on the ears of the Highlander). As time progressed, and the Westie assumed its autonomy, heads were modified and forefaces shortened to more closely approach the earlier progenitors of both breeds. The ultimate effects of the change has been one of the major differences between the two breeds, since the Scottie continued on the other road and today we find this breed with quite long heads, entirely unlike the Westie and Cairn branches of the basic blood.

From a background of proven facts, unsubstantiated statements, and subtle conjecture, we have the Westie of today: bred to the color of white, maintained in a small package, possessed of a great heart and a friendly air, an ideal companion for all occasions. He has all the desirable points of other Scotch breeds of dog without any of their drawbacks. The Westie is a great combination of fun, affection, and intelligence. Anyone who is once the owner of a Westie is always an enthusiastic booster of the breed.

The West Highlander is not an argumentative Terrier but is a plucky individual who will not back down and who will stand against a larger animal in matters of moral rights. He is fun loving, enjoying a play indoors or an outdoor hike or swim with equal vigor, entering into these endeavors with unfailing energy and great determination. While the Westie is as Scotch as a bagpipe, he lacks that extreme dourness so characteristic of other

"Boidheach," an early favorite of Col. Malcolm.

breeds of Scotch dogs. He lives with equal happiness indoors or out and displays his devotion with a grateful tongue and wagging tail that never fail to pay homage to his master. In all, a Westie is everything you can desire in a dog. The indomitable spirit of the breed is best exemplified by the following statement made by one of its host of admirers, "NO WATER WAS EVER TOO COLD AND NO EARTH WAS EVER TOO DEEP FOR THEM"—a fitting tribute to a grand dog.*

* Capt. Mackie, *Dogs of Scotland*, 1891

An early West Highland and a Scottish Terrier, showing long heads.
Note the ear pigmentation on the Westie.

38

The West Highland White Terrier in Ring and Kennel

The first dog shows held in England did not include Terriers on the agenda. In fact, no show record can be found before 1860 which mentioned the earth dogs. In that year, an exhibition held at Birmingham included a classification for "Scotch Terriers," and listed among the winners in that class were a "white Skye" and an "imported Skye." The 1863 show in London helped to further complicate the situation with classes for Skyes, "White Scotch," "Fawn Scotch," and "Blue Scotch," while other contemporary events divided some of these classes by weight, and by "cut" and "uncut" ears (the "uncut" ears frequently being dropped or semi-erect). The first show held in Scotland was staged in Glasgow in 1871 and classified six Terrier breeds, including Scotch Terriers.

In 1899 an effort was made to gain separate classes for "White Scottish Terriers." This appeared in the form of a request to the Kennel Club (English) by the White Scottish Terrier Club which registered its title with the Kennel Club on December 5 of that year. The request was denied on July 3, 1900 and the embryo club apparently disbanded since further notice of it cannot be found.*

From this confusion the breed emerged as the Poltalloch Terrier at Edinburgh in the early 1900's, and the first stable specialty club was formed in 1904 as the West Highland White Terrier Club of Scotland with the Duke of Argyll as its president. Following this activity the great Crufts show in England listed classes for the West Highland White Terrier in 1907. The same year, the English Kennel Club included the breed in the *English Kennel Club Calendar and Stud Book,* noting support by the West Highland White Terrier Club of England with D. T. McNeill its secretary and the Countess of Aberdeen its president. No dogs were registered in 1907, but in the following year 141 Highlanders made the pages.

While the breed had its beginnings in Scotland, the United States was not far behind in recognizing its virtues. In 1906, the Westminster Kennel Club had classes for Roseneath Terriers and five were on the bench, with Mrs. H. M. Harriman's Peter the Great (not registered) taking best. Peter continued to rule the breed at Westminster for the next two years.

It was not until 1908 that the American Kennel Club listed the breed in the Stud Book as a Roseneath Terrier, with the dog Talloch, #116076, owned by Mrs. Clinton Bell of Springfield, Mass., being the first to gain recognition. Thereafter, on May 31, 1909, the name of the breed was changed officially to West Highland White Terrier in the records of the American Kennel Club. The West Highland White Terrier of America was formed and admitted to membership in The American Kennel Club the following year (September 21st, 1909), with George Lauder as its first secretary. The Standard of the breed, patterned after the English Standard, was adopted on December 21, 1909. These early acts in Scotland, England, and the United States were the real beginning of the Westie fortunes and mark important milestones in the progress of the breed.

In England, we find that the 1908 English *Calendar* listed the first Westies to gain the necessary challenge certificates to

* *The Kennel Club etc.* by Jacquet, 1909, pp. 249, 267

A West Highland of the turn of the Century is the subject of this 1905 canvas by the famous animal artist Maud Earl. The painting was owned by the late Mrs. B. G. Frame.

Ch. Morven, possibly the most important of all early stud dogs in England, whelped 1905.

become champions. These were Ch. Morven (by Brogach ex Culaig), whelped March 28, 1905, a dog owned by Colin Young; Ch. Cromar Snowflake (by Morven ex Snowdrift) and Ch. Oronsay (by Conas ex Jean), both of which were owned by the Countess of Aberdeen. Snowdrift, the dam of Snowflake, was sired by Brogach out of Cona, which demonstrates an early and successful use of line breeding.

While little notice of the breed can be found in the United States prior to the 1908 date listed above, it is evident that white dogs of the general stamp were known and cherished for many years before the beginning of the twentieth century. This statement is based upon a Currier and Ives print in the author's possession titled, "The Watchers." (see page 4) The print was made sometime before 1872 as determined by the address thereon. While the proportions leave something to be desired, the dog is unquestionably a Highlander and proves beyond doubt that such dogs were known in America at a very early date.

In the United States, the English import Ch. Cream of the Skies, A.K.C. #124682, became—in 1909—the first of the breed to gain a U.S. championship. This dog was previously known in England as Clonmel Cream of the Skyes. George Lauder registered the first American-bred dog in 1909 when Glenailort Brogach gained A.K.C. #132845, although this Westie was by no means the first American-bred. That honor goes to a litter bred by Humphrey and Boyer of Mt. Kisco, N.Y., which was appropriately whelped on July 4, 1909. The litter was by Tighabruaich Glenailort, A.K.C. #121224, a Westminster winner in 1909, out of Shy Lady, A.K.C. #124681. The four dogs in this litter, registered in 1910, carried the rather prosaic names of Comet, #135701; Ikey, #135702; Little Eva, #135703 and White Cloud, #135704.

Also recorded in 1910 was the first Canadian-bred registered in the United States—a dog named Brose, A.K.C. #136107, whelped September 6, 1909, and owner-bred by Miss Ida W. Eadie of Montreal. While surveying the records of 1910, we also find two more champions of record, Ch. Barlae Snowflake,

A revealing collection of old English champions, circa 1910.

43

#136071 (by Master Hector ex Hawkhill Snowflake) , and Ch. Baughfell Talisker, #136070 (by Ballach Bhan ex Teorlig) . Both were owned by A. Albright of Newark, N.J. After these meager beginnings the breed began to expand rapidly, and each succeeding year brought out more fine West Highland White Terriers.

A history of the Highlander would be incomplete without review of some of the more famous English dogs of yesteryear. Champion Morven, previously mentioned, is said to have been the greatest single early influence on the breed.* His sire, Brogach, was a biggish dog of tremendous bone and substance, and his dam, Culaig, was known for her grand turn of body. The result of this union was evident for many years, as Morven sired Atholl, who produced Ch. Glenmhor Model, said to be Morven's best grandson. Other widely known dogs of this time included Ch. Kiltie, the Countess of Aberdeen's Ch. Oronsay, Mr. Holland Buckley's Ch. Nevis, Ballach Bhan, Inverailort Roy, and Dazzler Sands. Model, Kiltie, and Dazzler Sands were exported to the United States.

During the years that followed, many outstanding dogs were produced, a few of which were: Mrs. Kerr's Ch. Harviestoun Mab; Mrs. Clare's Ch. Cairn Ransa; Mrs. Buckley's Ch. White Sylvia; Mrs. Cyril Pacey's Chs. Wolvey Peacock and Wolvey Pepper; Mrs. E. O. Innes' Ch. Brean Glunyieman; Miss Hilda Shaw's Chs. Columbine Cilean and Cariad; Miss Thornton's Ch. Leeside Larkspur; Miss Smith-Woods' Chs. Ray and Roderick of Rushmoor; Mrs. Hewson's Chs. Clint Cheek and Clint Cocktail; Mrs. Allom's Furzefield Prosper; and Mrs. Bird's Ch. Placemore Caution and Miss Turnbull's fine sire, Ch. Leal Flurry. These were all dogs of note before World War II.

It would be anti-climatic not to mention Mrs. Pacey's pre-potent stud, Ch. Wolvey Patrician. This dog was one of the ring "greats" of his day but is better remembered as the sire of the incomparable Ch. Ray of Rushmoor and the grandsire of Ch. Wolvey Poacher, two of the most important stud forces of the past. A full history of the Wolvey Kennels, and a short

* *The West Highland White,* by Holland Buckley, 1911

44

Mrs. C. C. Pacey with a group of her Terriers. Left to right, Eng. Ch. Wolvey Pintail, Eng. Ch. Wolvey Wings, Eng. Ch. Wolvey Prefect, Eng. Ch. Wolvey Poacher and Eng. Ch. Wolvey Peacock. Photograph taken in 1936.

Ch. Pamela of Hillandale with Phil Prentice, handler, and Mrs. C. M. Bird
(of Placemore), judge, winning the specialty show in 1949.

biography of its owner, will be found in the chapter on Post War Activities in Britain.

The advent of World War II stifled the interest in shows in the United States. It also caused a slowdown in the breeding activities of many kennels, and importation was all but stopped. While shows were held, they were reduced in number and the fancy dwindled in size and virility. With the coming of peace, interest quickly regained its old fervor and breeding activity began to increase. Due to the partial depletion of breeding stock, some new blood was brought from Britain to aid in re-establishing the firm groundwork so necessary if any breed is to succeed. Early post—war imports included Mrs. Eppley's (formerly Mrs. John G. Winant) Chs. Cruben Cranny of Edgerstoune and Pamela of Hillandale; Captain Joseph Strokirk's Ch. Colin of Whitehills; and Mrs. A. S. Monroney's Ch. Hookwood Showman. These were the first imports to acquire the U.S. title after cessation of hostilities.

As we pass to the West Highland White Terrier in the United States, we find a long and varied history replete with the names of great imports and well represented by a host of outstanding homebreds. Mr. Robert Geolet's Glenmere Kennels with Chs. Maister, Rumpus of Glenmere, and the aforementioned Kiltie, together with the Conejo Kennels of Mrs. Roy Rainey, headed by Ch. Dunvegan Hero, were responsible for much of the early ring success of the breed. The Ayre, Braewood, Greentree, Knoll, Endcliffe, and Strathspey Kennels were also active during the first twenty years of this century, but all of these pioneer establishments are now out of existence.

Several famous kennels, some of which are now closed, deserve special mention in view of their extended activities and the fact that dogs bearing their affixes were or are so widely known.

The first of these is the Nishkenon Kennels of Mr. and Mrs. W. B. Rogers of Sherborn, Massachusetts. Although this insti-

Ch. Rosstor Raith, Rosstor homebred.

Ch. Rosstor Rajus

Ch. Rosstor the De'il

48

tution flourished more than twenty years ago, the impact of its efforts is still felt in the breed. "Nishkenon" is an Indian name signifying "of the mists" and was also the name of the Rogers' estate situated on the banks of the Lake of the Mists.

Nishkenon imported the best for foundation stock and brought to these shores some of the finest English dogs of the day. Patriarch of the kennel was Ch. White Adonis, a New York winner. His son Ch. Nishkenon Rogue did well in the ring, while his daughter Ch. Nishkenon Wee Lass upheld the distaff side of the ledger. Ch. Crivoch Clashmore of Nishkenon and Ch. Maulden Scamp of Nishkenon were two top studs. But of all the inmates of the kennel, Ch. White Cloud of Nishkenon probably took top billing. She won her championship in record time and topped off the performance with a Terrier Group win and an award for best bitch in show in the days when Westie wins of this caliber were unheard-of. These are but a few of the many champions owned by the kennel but serve to demonstrate, in a small way, the quality of the inmates.

Much credit should go to Nishkenon for a well-balanced and properly executed breeding program. The Rogers were "real dog people" and not only helped the Westie but also the pure-bred dog. In this direction, Mr. Rogers served as an officer in several kennel clubs and was a director of The American Kennel Club. His great interest in dogs finally led him to take residence in Grand Junction, Tennessee, where he was president of the National Field Trial Association for many years.

Rosstor is another famous name—famous in West Highland Whites and equally famous in dogs. The kennel has housed (in addition to Westies) Greyhounds, Scottish Terriers, and Wire Haired Fox Terriers. The Westie activity commenced about 1913 with the acquisition of Ch. Walpole Witty.* Later came such greats as Ch. Walpole Winter and Ch. Cairn Ransa. Probably the most widely known of its dogs was an import, Ch. Clark's Hill Snooker. This establishment also bred many fine Westies, including Ch. Rosstor Riatt, Ch. Rosstor Roderick, and Ch. Rosstor Raven. These last three were among the many dogs

---

* Pure-bred Dogs—American Kennel Gazette, February 1927, page 9 et seq.

Captain Chipman's two great ones: Eng. and Am. Ch. Wolvey Pandora (left) and Wolvey Poet (right).

Eng. and American Ch. Brisk of Branston of Edgerstoune, imported and originally owned by Mrs. Winant and subsequently acquired by the author. He was bred by Mrs. D. M. Dennis and was a full brother to Ch. Barrister of Branston.

that went to the Edgerstoune Kennels in 1929 when Miss Claudia Phelps dispersed the West Highland Whites. Incidentally several other breeds were retained. At the time, Miss Phelps issued a sixteen page brochure giving photos, descriptions and show records of some eight champions, including Chs. Clark's Hill Snooker together with Chum of Childwick, Rosstor the De'il, Rosstor Raith and Rosstor Rajus together with some 35 others, several of which were subsequently made titleholders. Many other Rosstor homebreds were widely known and subsequently found their way into kennels of new enthusiasts who made good use of the fine bloodlines in establishing their own foundation stock.

Another kennel of long standing, closed following on the death of its owner, was Charan. Located at Madison, Connecticut, it was a joint venture of Captain and Mrs. H. E. H. Chipman. Here, many Westies were bred, and, as late as 1948, when I visited the kennel, Highlanders by scores scampered through the woods after unwary rabbits or barked at the base of trees at more timid squirrels. Captain Chipman believed in raising his dogs naturally and they thrived in this environment.

Charan was one of the two large kennels in this country whose bloodlines were based primarily on the Wolvey Poacher branch of the Patrician line. Poacher blood was brought in through an import, English and American Ch. Wolvey Poet of Charan. He, in turn, sired Ch. Charan Minstrel, who was sold to W. A. Tyler. English and American Ch. Wolvey Pandora of Charan was another notable of the kennel, while Ch. Charan Merry Whimsy, a homebred, helped make history for Charan.

The kennel was particularly active in the ring during the twenties and thirties, when it gained wide acclaim. Even as late as 1950, Capt. Chipman brought dogs to the shows and was always an interested spectator, well-known to all.

Probably the largest and most successful kennel of Westies in this country began operations in the late twenties when Mrs. Marion Eppley (then Mrs. John G. Winant) brought the Highlander to Edgerstoune. The perennial success of this es-

51

Ch. Edgerstoune Roughy

Ch. Edgerstoune Rastus

Ch. Edgerstoune Rowdy

Wolvey Plainsman of Springmeade

tablishment is attested by more than fifty champions, imports and homebreds, that gained the title under the kennel's colors from its inception in New Hampshire until its closing at Valley Cottage, New York, in 1954. At this point, it is only fitting to say that Edgerstoune's early efforts included Dalmatians, while its later efforts were divided between the West Highlander and the Scottish Terrier, and that equal success was attained in both breeds.

Edgerstoune obtained some of its foundation stock from the Rosstor Kennels, as previously mentioned. This was augmented with a host of imports that eventually gave the kennel one of the strongest groups in the breed. Some of the early imports included English Ch. Cooden Stonechat, English Ch. Crivoch Candida, Cooden Sliko, Ch. Wolvey Pattern of Edgerstoune, Ch. Clint Cocktail, and Ch. Ray of Rushmoor.

Homebreds were legend, with such stalwarts as Ch. Edgerstoune Radium (an outstanding stud), Ch. Edgerstoune Roughy, and Ch. Edgerstoune Royalty, to name a few. In more recent years, Ch. Cruben Cranny of Edgerstoune, Ch. Pamela of Hillandale, Ch. Brisk of Branston of Edgerstoune, Ch. Cruben Crystal, Ch. Edgerstoune Valley Belle, and Ch. Edgerstoune White Raider carried the banner into the ring.

Mrs. Eppley used an unusual method to raise her homebreds. Puppies were always an operation unto themselves. Mrs. Fred Leonard was, for many years, in charge of this phase of the work, and her efforts were certainly apparent. The older dogs and show stock were housed in a separate kennel with its own manager, who in most cases was also the show handler. Edgerstoune had the good fortune of having many fine handlers and managers in the persons of Harry Hardcastle, Bob Gorman, Jimmy Murphy, Joe Menary, and Cliff Hallmark. Phil Prentice also handled dogs for the kennel.

In any event, Mrs. Leonard's concentrated efforts on puppies paid off because the youngsters received more attention, and their dispositions developed well and reflected this attention.

The passing of the Edgerstoune Kennels was a great loss to the breed, since its fine stud dogs made available to the fancy

53

Ch. Robinridge Countess

Ch. Wolvey Pace of Edgerstoune

Ch. Cooden Sheriff of Edgerstoune

Ch. Springmeade Rexminimus

54

the best of domestic and imported bloodlines from which to choose, and use.

The success of the kennel can be attributed in a large measure to Mrs. Eppley's astute ability to pick a winner, at home or abroad. This was well demonstrated by the way she acquired two of her best. Some years ago, she judged a show in England and placed a Westie bitch best in the show. Immediately after the judging, she bought the bitch and brought her back to this country. The acquisition was Ch. Wolvey Pattern of Edgerstoune, who went best in show at Westminster in 1942, the first Westie ever to win this high honor. Years later, the same situation was repeated. Again in England, Mrs. Eppley placed a Scottish Terrier best in show and then bought the dog, Ch. Walsing Winning Trick of Edgerstoune. Of course, it is history now, but Trick subsequently emulated Pattern and gained the pinnacle at Westminster in 1950. So twice Mrs. Eppley placed a dog best in show in England and twice she backed up her decision by buying the dog and then winning top honors with her purchase in the United States.

Springmeade is still another kennel with many years of experience and is owned by Miss Marguerite Van Schaick. This lady's first interest was in Collies, but she soon transferred her affections to the Highlander. Early purchases included a granddaughter of English Ch. Morven and a puppy by Ch. Rumpus of Glenmere from the kennels of Robert Geolet. The active start of her kennel came when she acquired Ch. Ardoch Chief from the Conejo Kennels of Mrs. Rainey, and in 1917 Springmeade was registered in her name and began earnest operations in the breed which have continued until the present.

According to Miss Van Schaick, Ch. Reaside Rex, an import, was her top dog, for he sired Ch. Springmeade Rexminimus, Ch. Springmeade Black Eyed Susan, and others that gained fame in the ring. Rexminimus gave her the greatest thrill when he won the breed and placed in the Group at the age of ten, showing that Westies are ageless. The Springmeade Highlanders have always been handled by either their owner or by Charles Trayford, who, at one time, was in charge of Conejo Kennels.

55

Ch. Hookwood Showman, owned by
Mrs. A. S. Monroney.

Ch. Heather Hill David

Ch. Robinridge MacBeth

The Springmeade dogs have been instrumental in the beginnings of many kennels, such as the See-Are Kennels of film star Charles Ruggles, who purchased two champions from Springmeade, while Ch. Springmeade Sheila, a daughter of Wolvey Plainsman, was one of the foundations of the kennel of Miss Marguerite Vance in the Midwest.

The Heather Hill Kennels of Mrs. William Dexter showed to advantage for many years. Some of the most successful bloodlines of this kennel were based on the Wolvey Poacher line through two of his sons, Ch. Heather Hill David and Ch. Heather Hill Patrick. Other widely known inmates included the bitch Ch. Heather Hill Nora, Wolvey Playfellow of Heather Hill, and Ch. Cooden Skua of Heather Hill. These and a host of others kept the kennel in the forefront of the fancy for many years.

Mrs. A. S. Monroney's Robinridge Kennels was another in the long list of successful establishments that bears mention. It was responsible for such homebreds as Ch. Robinridge MacBeth, Ch. Robinridge Breathless, and Ch. Robinridge Cherie. Its imports include Ch. Hookwood Showman, who had an all too short career following World War II, and Ch. Culbahn White Ribbon of Robinsridge.

Mrs. Monroney often used Dorothy Hardcastle, daughter of the aforementioned Harry Hardcastle as a handler. It is interesting to note that Mrs. Monroney still has a vital interest in the breed and had an entry at the 1975 Montgomery County Kennel Club show.

Several other widely known kennels, now inactive, were the Belmertle Kennels of D. A. Tyler, who owned Ch. Charan Minstrel; the Hobscot Kennels of Mr. and Mrs. C. A. Hobbs, with a good winner in Ch. Hobscot Son of Mac; the Donald McKay Smiths' Rothmore Kennels, with Ch. Mheall Dirk; and the aforementioned See-Are Kennels of Charles Ruggles.

Among later entries in the field were: Miss Marguerite Vance of Indianapolis with a strong kennel that included Ch. Battison Beacon, a leading stud force bred by the late Edward Danks (Battison), a life-time breeder (Beacon was responsible for a

Ch. Cruben Silver Birk, owned by Mrs. Anthony M. Walters.

Ch. Billikin, owned by Mrs. Anthony M. Walters, was familiar to thousands of fanciers for many years as the masthead dog on the Westie column in *Pure-Bred Dogs —American Kennel Gazette.*

Ch. Tyndrum Morar, owned and bred by Mrs. Anthony Walters.

number of the good dogs shown during the late forties); Mr. Perry Chadwick's Inverary Kennels, owner of Ch. Highland Ursa Major and Ch. Wolvey Parole among others. Inverary is no longer active, although the dogs made a great name for the establishment in its heyday; Mrs. Anthony Walter, owner of the Tyndrum Kennels and Chs. Cruben Silver Birk, Billikin, Mallaig Brilliant Monarch, Tyndrum Dirk, and Tyndrum Morar.

Mrs. Walters holds the distinction of owning and exhibiting the winning Terrier brace at Westminster in 1962, topping all Terrier entries in the competition. This made a clean sweep for the breed since Ch. Elfinbrook Simon captured the group and best in show. It is believed that this was the first and only time that Highlanders won the brace competition. Mrs. Walters continues to be active, both in breeding and in the ring so that Tyndrum now assumes the position of being one of the oldest, active American Kennels in the breed with close to forty years of effort.

Mrs. R. K. Mellon owned the Rachelwood Kennels, the home of many fine imports and breeder of a host of dogs that made their mark, always with Andy DeGraw on the lead. Included were the likes of: Chs. Hookwood Marquis, Hookwood Twinkle Bavena of Branston, Rachelwood Radiance and Briarrose of Branston; Mr. and Mrs. John T. Marvin, whose Cranbourne Kennels were active until about 1966 and who bred and exhibited more best in show dogs than any other domestic establishment to date, with Chs. Cranbourne Arial, Cranbourne Atomic and Cranbourne Alexandrite to its credit.

This brings us to the Wishing Well Kennels started by Mrs. Florence Worcester and her daughter Barbara. Begun in about 1950, it grew rapidly and imported some of the best that England had to offer. Ch. Cruben Melphis Chloe was the first big winner, followed by her son, Ch. Cruben Dextor (who proved to be a top flight show dog and an even greater sire), his son Ch. Tulyar of Trenean, Ch. Cruben Flashback, Ch.

59

Symmetra Snip and the celebrated campaigner, Ch. Elfinbrook Simon, a top winner and the breed's all-time top sire. In 1963 Miss Worcester married Henry Sayres, a life-long Terrier man, and the kennels were moved from New Jersey to Malibu, California. The transfer did not affect the quality of the dogs as additional toppers continued to make their appearance in the ring under the Wishing Well banner. A listing of a few of these, in more or less chronological order, includes; Ch. Whitebriar Journeyman (owned jointly with Sally Hudson); Ch. Rainsborowe Redvers, a good winner; Ch. Snowcliff Patrician; Ch. Royal Tartan Glen O'Red Lodge (owned jointly with Richard M. Hilliker); Ch. Famecheck Platinum; and Ch. Lymehills Birkfell Solstice, who finished quickly in early 1969.

Other Wishing Well notables include Ch. Famecheck Busy Body; Ch. Keithall Marksman and the steady winner, Ch. Pinmoney Puck shown so successfully by Cliff Hallmark and upon retirement going into the kennels of Mrs. M. Schiele under joint ownership. In 1973, Kristajen Krackerjack was imported and made his title quickly in California competition. Shortly thereafter, in 1974, Wishing Well came back East and relocated in New Jersey where it had begun. Its owner had married Edward Keenan, himself interested in the breed but many things had changed. Henry Sayres succumbed in 1970, a great loss to the fancy in general and Terriers in particular. Additionally, Mrs. Florence Worcester died suddenly in 1974 shortly after coming back East. She was a grand lady and a steadying influence on the breed. These deaths deprived the Highlander of both support and knowledge. Today, Wishing Well is still active but on a greatly reduced scale to that of the early sixties. Mrs. Keenan is engaged presently in judging the breed and other Terriers, a vocation for which she has had the best of training through contact with some of the top dogs of the times. This is but a partial inventory of the many fine Highlanders that have been owned and shown by this extensive kennel. While most of the dogs mentioned have been imports, a host of homebreds have also come from its pens and

Eng. and Am. Ch. Wolvey Philippa
of Clairedale

Eng., Can., and Am. Ch. Cruben
Melphis Chloe

Ch. Hookwood Banneret, owned by
Mrs. Richard K. Mellon.

Ch. Hookwood Marquis, also owned
by Mrs. Mellon.

today we find a number of dogs around the country co-owned by Wishing Well and others. Scores of American-breds have made their titles bearing the Wishing Well prefix. Chs. Wishing Well Brigadoon and Ch. Wishing Well's White Frost, owned by Mr. and Mrs. Eugene B. Clifford, bear special mention in this category. Surely, to date, Wishing Well has been the most successful of all American Kennels.

No exposition of Wishing Well would be complete without an added mention of the greatness of its bellwether, Ch. Elfinbrook Simon. While his show and stud records will be elaborated upon in other sections of this book, one cannot overlook the impact his presence had upon the breed. Until 1962, the Highlander had been gaining by small increments in the general plan among all breeds of dog. After Simon's triumph at Westminster that year, coupled with his victorious campaigning around the country, the growth of the breed became dramatic. Every year since the happy event, the Westie has added supporters who have made the upswing in breed position both numerically and quality-wise phenomenal. Too much credit cannot be given to the dog. It is interesting to note here that Simon was brought out for a final showing at the California Specialty show in 1968, after several years of retirement, and although nine years old, looked and acted like a youngster. He captured best of breed from the Veteran's class, demonstrating once again the ageless quality of a fine dog. Simon died in 1970.

Another large establishment that deserves mention for its many efforts towards breed improvement is the Clairedale Kennels of the late Mrs. Claire Dixon. This name had been widely known for at least four decades through its success in many breeds including Chow Chows, Airedales, Sealyhams, and Welsh Terriers. Mrs. Dixon added Westies to the pens in about 1951 and quickly built a strong force in the breed. Among the best known were: Ch. Hookwood Smartie, Ch. Wolvey Piquet, Ch. Scoram Maybelle, Ch. Cruben Moray, and Ch. Crinan Hector, all carrying the of Clairedale suffix. With this fine beginning, the kennel plans began to materialize and Ch. Clairedale Greetings was one of the first homebreds to win well.

Ch. Wishing Well's White Frost, owned by
Mr. and Mrs. Eugene Clifford.

Ch. Rannoch-Dune Defiance.

Ch. Edgerstoune Requa

Eng. and Am. Ch. Wolvey Piquet
of Clairedale

Ch. Rannoch-Dune Dixie

Unfortunately for the breed, Mrs. Dixon died in 1959 and activities were quickly and sharply curtailed. The establishment was continued on a reduced basis by a daughter, Mrs. Vojvoda although Westies eventually were dropped from the plan. Fortunately, another daughter, Mrs. Peggy Newcombe, who was often seen showing the Clairedale dogs, added the Highlander to her famous Pennyworth Kennels and thus continued the family interest in the breed. Mrs. Newcombe's last big winner was the import, Ch. Incheril Ishca of Pennyworth, who captured the breed at the 1969 National specialty show.

Several persons widely known through the years but no longer highly active merit mention at this time. These include: Miss Dorothy Hardcastle, daughter of Harry Hardcastle, who still has a great interest in the breed although not actively breeding Westies at this time; the late Mrs. J. Haskell, owner of the highly respected Lawenton Kennels, a long-term devotee of the Westie; Mrs. Rachael Sangster, early supporter, who has long since dropped from an active role as have Miss Jane Peters and Miss Louise Lang. These persons are mentioned because they all had an influence upon our breed. It was their interest and devotion coupled with that of the many others mentioned earlier that brought the Highlander along (slowly, to be sure), that protected the quality of the breed, and that made possible the tremendous upsurge that we have today. Without a solid foundation of quality stock, such growth would not have been possible.

There are a number of others. This group includes the late Mrs. B. G. Frame of Indianapolis. Mrs. Frame's Wigtown establishment was in existence since the war until her untimely death in 1975 gaining in stature each passing year. She had shown dogs of her own as well as in co-ownership with Mrs. E. P. McCarty, where the prefix used was Wigmac (a combination of Wigtown and Mac-A-Dac, Mrs. McCarty's prefix). Ch. Wigtown Talent Scout was her initial big winner, a dog that did well for the breed both in the ring and at stud. However the dynamic force was surely Ch. Rannoch Dune Down Beat. He was purchased from

Mrs. Frank Brumby and has been shown to advantage for several years. In 1969 he brought his overall total to 25 best in shows and surpassed the enviable record made by Simon. In addition, he has been a consistent group winner with 99 group firsts to his credit. Down Beat was shown initially by Florise Hogan, but the majority of his top triumphs have been under the guidance of George Ward, the same handler that carried Simon to his great record. Down Beat dominated the breed at the shows from 1965 through 1968 in the same manner that Simon did during his three-year-span from 1960 through 1962.

After Down Beat retired, Mrs. Frame imported the dog, Purston Pinmoney Pedlar from M. Collings of England. This dog was given to George Ward and proved to be a winner from the start. He captured some 48 best in show awards and 109 groups during his career that spanned several years and in 1973 led all Terriers in top triumphs. The "Pedlar dog" as Mrs. Frame called him, was indeed a laster and brought great acclaim to the breed with his many top wins.

Mrs. McCarty has also made a mark in the history of the Highlander. Possibly the two best known of her entries were the bitches, Chs. Mac-A-Dac Mistletoe and Mac-A-Dac Highland Kilts. Each led the sex in show wins during the years 1966 and 1967 respectively.

Few establishments have had the constant success in breeding enjoyed by Rannoch Dune, owned by Mrs. Frank Brumby. The establishment was located originally on Long Island but has since moved to Arizona where it continues to thrive. Committed in the main to American-bred dogs of its own breeding, the yearly results are most satisfying and constant.

Begun shortly after the war, Mrs. Brumby has brought the program along slowly and surely to produce the best in quality. Chs. Rannoch Dune Duke, Rannoch Dune Destry, and Rannoch Dune Demon have all done well at stud. Demon sired such outstanding dogs as, Chs. Rannoch Dune Duke, Destry, Dante and Dominie and is assured immortality as the sire of Rannoch Dune Down Beat. Duke, of course has many titleholders to his credit

Winners at 1957 West Highland White Terrier Club of America Specialty Show. Left to right: Tom Adams with his Roseneath White Knight, best of breed; Mrs. Worcester, Club president; Mrs. William Dexter, judge; and Andy DeGraw handling Ch. Hookwood Twinkle.

Ch. Cruben Moray of Clairedale winning the West Highland White Terrier Club of America 1958 Specialty Show. Left to right: Mrs. William Worcester, Club president; Bob Gorman, handler; and Mrs. John T. Marvin, judge.

as have several others in the long list of dogs bred at Rannoch Dune. The kennels are extensive and have a steady breeding program that brings out a never-ending supply of winners.

Mr. and Mrs. Robert Lowry's Maxwelton Kennels in Aurora, Mo. has carved a niche in the modern history of the breed, steadily breeding quality animals that have done well at the shows. Maxwelton had the good fortune of importing that grand show and brood bitch, Ch. Donark Dancer in the early 1950s. She, by the great Eng. Ch. Shiningcliff Simon, did well at the shows (won two best in shows) and became the dam of seven Maxwelton titleholders. The Lowrys have followed a well conceived and carefully executed plan of breeding that melds the best in domestic and imported bloodlines and has produced a steady outflow of titleholders including two best in show winners to date.

The late Doris Eisenberg of California got her foundation stock from Mrs. Frame, and her Kar-Ric Kennels came a long way in a relatively short time. The brood matron, Ch. Wigtown Margene, produced five titleholders for her, which have been used well in the overall program to conceive eight additional champions. Some of her best were Chs. Kar-Ric's Rainsborowe Replica, Kar-Ric's Top of the Morning (now owned by Mrs. B. Poueymirou) and the Canadian-bred Ch. Dreamland's Happy Mick (co-owned with Mrs. N. Alexander). The record of this kennel during the comparatively brief length of its activity demonstrates that intelligent breeding with an open mind can bring both rapid and satisfying results.

Another highly successful breeder living in New Jersey is Mrs. Triskett Vogelius who, though operating on a relatively small scale, has produced and won well with her homebreds. Ch. Triskett's Most Happy Fella has been a good producer as well as a winner in the ring and Ch. Triskett's My Fair Lady also bears mention in view of her success in a relatively limited show career. Both have captured high honors at specialty and all-

Ch. Slitrig Shandy.

Ch. Wolvey Pickwick.

breed events. More lately, Ch. Battison Belladona completed her title in good company, and such dogs as Chs. Triskett's Topper and Topnotcher have also made the grade.

Mrs. E. K. Fischer of Chicago is another who had good success. She purchased one of her first Westies from Mrs. Frame. Subsequently, she went to Mrs. Pacey for advice and dogs, and obtained Ch. Wolvey Pickwick in the package. This move paid big dividends since Pickwick did very well at the shows and claimed the top prize at both Stone City in 1963 and Milwaukee in 1964. At this point, another mid-Westerner must be mentioned. Mrs. C. C. Fawcett, with her widely known artist husband "Tex," comes from Kirkwood, Mo. and while no newcomer to dogs, she first took up Westies in about 1956. In the intervening years she has done well both in the Obedience and conformation rings, where she exhibits the Forest Glen dogs all over the land. During the period of her tenure in the breed her accomplishments have been many. A respectable number of titleholders have come from the kennel's pens, generally exhibited by their owner. Ch. Forest Glen Simon Sez Be Brisk, a son of Elfinbrook Simon, gave her the most satisfying triumph when he placed best in show at Columbia, Mo. in 1966.

Returning to the West Coast, one finds the activities of the late Margaret Jensen's Marjen Highlanders spanned several years through which many fine imports and American-breds carried the colors. One of her memorable imports was Ch. Rainsborowe Redvers, subsequently owned and campaigned by Wishing Well. However, Ch. Famecheck Viking stands out above all others and brings the kennel into sharp focus, for he was shown extensively on the coast and won well. To me, his most notable achievement was the double victory at New York in 1963 when at the age of nine and a half years he captured best of breed at both the national breed specialty and Westminster amid the best of competition. The dog showed to perfection for handler Daisy Austad and the placements were enthusiastically received.

Another Californian, Mrs. Willard Boston, brought her Loch-

Ch. Famecheck Viking, a specialty and Westminster winner at nine-and-a-half years.

Ch. Rainsborowe Redvers, with his handler Henry J. Sayres.

Ch. Triskett's Most Happy Fella, owned, bred and handled by Triskett Vogelius.

glen Kennels into contention with several fine English imports including the littermates Lochglen Haigus and Lochglen Lorrel, together with their dam, Rivelin Rosary, who was brought over in whelp. All are now champions. The kennel was moved East for a few years which caused a temporary setback in plans, but is now re-established in California. Later titleholders include Ch. Lochglen Druid, a Haigus son, and Ch. Lochglen Inka, Druid's daughter.

A Michigan kennel that did well during the late fifties and early sixties was Mrs. Robert Goddard's Kirkaldy group. It owned many fine dogs and in 1962 captured the fall specialty show with Ch. Rhinafa The Rock. Mrs. Goddard was the ultimate owner of Ch. Tulyar of Trenean and used him to good effect during the waning years of his career. Here was a breeder who made use of the best in domestic and imported blood which results in a well balanced and productive kennel. While in the Midwest a word must be said about the long-standing activities of Mrs. S. M. Blue and her daughter, Mrs. Marion DeLuzansky (Klintilloch). Both began their interest in the breed during the early forties and have produced consistently a long line of top Westies. Mrs. DeLuzansky handled Ch. Highland Ursa Major to many of his early triumphs and was one of the first to trim the breed to benefit its position. The kennel has bred two best in show dogs in Chs. Klintilloch Molly Dee and Klintilloch Mercator. Its studs, Chs. Klintilloch Mercury and Klintilloch Monopoly have done extremely well and have produced nine and eleven title-holders respectively to date to carry on the kennel's tradition of quality stock. Several years ago the establishment was moved to Arizona where it now operates.

Mr. Elsworth Howell, a life-time dog enthusiast came into the breed when he purchased the English import, Ch. Sollershott Sober. The dog had been a good winner before his expatriation and continued to win well for several years under the guidance of Mr. and Mrs. Forsyth. Sober captured several groups and an untold number of placements as he was campaigned through the years 1966–68. Indeed, he won more best of breeds than any other Highlander in both 1966 (61) and 1967 (37).

Ch. Sollershott Sober, pictured with handler Jane Forsyth. Owned by Elsworth S. Howell.

Ch. Mac-A-Dac Highland Kilts, with handler Florise Hogan. Owned by Mrs. E. P. McCarty.

Ch. Alpingay Impressario, a best in show winner, owned and handled by Mrs. G. F. Church.

Many other successful exhibitors have come to the fore in recent years through the winnings of their dogs. In this group are Dr. Lois Dickie, of Pennsylvania, whose Ch. Alderbrook Jolly Roger has been a consistent winner for several years, climaxing his efforts with a 1968 best in show; the Herman Felltons of Georgia, long Afghan breeders and exhibitors of note, but who never owned a Highlander until they purchased the dog, Ch. Whitebriar Jalisker. His accomplishments under the guidance of Mrs. "Mike" Leathers have been little short of sensational, bringing him to a record of 11 all-breed bests in show and many groups through 1968; Mrs. Ida Weaver of Washington State, owned numerous fine Highlanders but her import, Ch. Ugadale Artist's Model topped the list and brought home a coveted best in show in 1968 to add to his accomplishments at stud. Mrs. Weaver is now deceased to the detriment of the breed although dogs of her breeding are still giving a good account of themselves. Miss Katharine Hayward (Huntinghouse Hill) of Rhode Island has been breeding Westies for many years, but until she brought out the homebred Ch. Huntinghouse Little Fella did not receive the publicity which she deserved. This one claimed the Newtown, Conn. event in 1968 to add to a long list of group wins and placements. He also topped the national specialty the same year. Miss Hayward is one of the breed's most respected fanciers and has served the Highlander well in many ways. It will be remembered that this same lady owned the import, Ch. Slitrig Shandy many years ago and did well, although nothing as sensational as with her homebred winners. Good fortune has also smiled upon the activities of Mrs. G. F. Church (Sinalco), St. Louis, Mo. She had been showing for several years and in 1967 brought out an import, Alpingay Impressario. He did well at the specialty and at Westminster and was then sent on the circuit where he was best in show twice in 1968 and again in 1969.

One of the 1960's imports to the American fancy was Miss Bergit Zakchewski. This young lady came to this country from England and brought a dog with her. The dog, Ch. Monsieur

Aus Der Flerlage, had been winning all over Europe and continued to win in this country. He completed his American title to add to his impressive list which includes championships in Germany, Mexico, Luxembourg, Czechoslovakia and England (where he went best in show at Belfast). In addition, he has qualified for many other European honors. He has been handled and conditioned by his proud owner to these many accomplishments and in 1969 added two American bests in show to his honors. Miss Zakchewski is now Mrs. Clay Coady.

Additionally, many others have done well with their dogs and deserve mention because of their sterling accomplishments, among them are; Florise Hogan (Flogan), the late Cecil Dingman (Blak-N-Wite), Mrs. L. L. Slygh (Elmview), Mrs. Ruth Birmingham (Lochcrest), Mrs. Dorothy Pubols (Mc Twiddles), Joseph and Donna Barber (breeder-owners of the multiple specialty winner, Ch. Glenhaven Caesar), Allan and Marlene Kotlisky (Wiloglen), successful with several top dogs, Joan Graber (Rudh're) with a host of steady winners, Neoma and Jim Eberhardt (Merryhart) of California, long-time advocates of the breed and most successful of late at specialty events, Mr. and Mrs. D. Mocabee (Happymac), another California couple that have done extremely well, Mrs. Harry Grindle (Mar'Grin), Dee and Dick Hanna (D and D) and, of course, Clifford Hallmark (Vimy Ridge), a professional handler who, with his family, is a successful breeder who has gained his greatest acclaim through the handling of other people's dogs. There are, of course, a host of others, many of whom are no longer actively engaged in either breeding or exhibiting. Of the newer converts, Mrs. Kate Seeman, long a devotee of the Border Terrier, has entered the lists as an exhibitor of the Highlander. Her Ch. Braidholme White Tornado of Binate was best in show at Montgomery County 1974 and her Ch. On Guard of Backmuir was group third at Westminster 1977. Mrs. Seeman's dogs are shown by Cliff Hallmark. Another establishment that is fast coming to the fore is Wetherside, owned by Mrs. Constance Jones. The dogs, again, are shown by Hallmark and include three best in show recipients, Chs. Pillerton Peterkin, Purston Polly Perkins and Commander of Tintibar. Coming into the show scene about the same time was Dr. A. T. Hunt (Bayou Glen) who had his first good winner in Ch. Highlands Angus. Angus was succeeded by Ch. Ardenrun 'Andsome of Purston who took the country by storm with a steady string of best in show awards from late 1974 to the conclusion of his career in 1976. Andy was shown by Dora Lee Wilson and made his most impressive wins, in the writer's opinion, at Westminster in 1975 when he placed at the top of a highly competitive Terrier group, only the third such placement in history for the breed and at Montgomery County in 1976 where he was best in show over the largest gathering of terriers in history. He had 37 group firsts in 1976 and won the Quaker Oats award for top terrier for the year. Dr. and Mrs. G. G. Meisels and their daughter-handler are steady exhibitors and have done well with their White Oaks dogs, especially with Ch. White Oaks Lover Boy, a best in show winner, as has Mrs. Joanne Glodek (Mak-Ken-Char) who had the thrill of seeing her Ch. Keithall Pilot go best in show in Puerto Rico with her daughter handling. Both combinations have demonstrated that youngsters with ability and a good dog can win in any company. Others worthy of mention are Mr. and Mrs. Tom Ward (Donnybrook), Shirley Jean O'Neill (Heritage Farm), the J. E. Craigmiles' Jolen dogs, Elaine Gnatowsky (Natos), C. W. Lewis (Nic Mac), F. and P. Sherman (Kirk O'The Glen), the Prosswick Highlanders of R. and M. Pross, N. and E. Gauthier's Skaket's dogs, Mr. and Mrs. Samuel Faust's Whytehavens, the James Finley's Woodlawn representatives, Diane and Helen Fronczak of Wyndergael, Jerry and Bobbe London with a good winner in Ch. London's Duffy Mac Duf, Bill Ferrara's and John Price's Biljonblue Kennels presently being expanded in view of a co-operative effort with Mrs. Kearsey and her Pillerton dogs (Mrs. Kearsey's credentials are discussed in detail in the chapter on English Kennels). The Biljonblue dogs have been much in evidence for some time and are now housed in new and expanded quarters in Emmaus, Pennsylvania. Ch. Biljonblue's Ali Baba is the current standard-bearer, together with a host of others. One can see the tremendous growth in interest in Westies that has been apparent during the sixties and seventies during a period when there has been a corresponding decrease in interest among earlier fanciers dating back to the war and before. This means that the broad cross section of the present group are relative newcomers in point of background although the numbers involved are far greater than ever before. For this reason, it has been impossible to list each and every serious breeder. Many additional names will be discovered in the kennel listings beginning on page 227 but even this tabulation is by no means complete. Suffice it to say, that the breed continues to be strong and is supported by a large group of serious and dedicated fanciers with the best interests of the West Highlander at heart. It is a most fortunate situation and one that should provide for a steady improvement in the overall quality of the breed for years to come.

Ch. Huntinghouse Little Fella, best in show winner, pictured with handler Roberta Krohne. Owned by Miss Katherine Hayward.

Ch. Ugadale Artist's Model, best in show winner, owned by the late Mrs. C. K. Weaver.

Ch. Wolvey Pattern of Edgerstoune winning best in show at Westminster in 1942. Left to right, Bob Gorman, handler, Gerald Livingston of the Westminster Kennel Club and H. E. Mellenthin, judge.

Ch. Elfinbrook Simon going Best in Show at Westminster in 1962. Left to right: William Rockefeller, Club president; George Ward, handler; Heywood Hartley, judge.

The Best in Show Winners

Top show wins (bests in show) are indicative of quality and the West Highland White Terrier through a number of fine specimens came into recognition early and continued to gain in stature as the years passed. The first best in show win was made by Ch. Clark's Hill Snooker at a Ladies Dog Club event many years ago. This triumph came before the day of recording top placements, so the exact records are not available except through the memories of old timers who verify the statement.

In more recent years, best in show awards have been divided between a number of Highlanders well spread around the land. The second such triumph went to Mrs. Eppley's English import Ch. Wolvey Pattern of Edgerstoune at the Manchester, N.H., show in 1940. And then, two years later, she made her great triumph at the 1942 Westminster Kennel Club event in New York. During the entire period, she was winning and placing in Terrier Groups.

At Hammond, Indiana, in 1944, Mr. Ben Gillette's American-bred Ch. Gillette's Lord Tuffington was the next show winner

79

Ch. Clark's Hill Snooker, credited as first Westie to win best in show in America.

Ch. Wigtown Talent Scout, show winner at Hodgensville, Ky., 1957. Judge, Hans Oberhammer; handler, Dick Cooper.

Ch. Highland Ursa Major winning his first best in show at Dayton in 1947. L. to r.: Mrs. Robert Miller, E. D. McQuown, and Mrs. Marion D'Luzansky.

Ch. Cruben Dextor, owned by Wishing Well Kennels, was a multiple best in show winner in the early 1950s. He also exerted a tremendous influence as a sire of quality that is strongly seen in the breed even today.

Ch. Klintilloch Molly Dee

Ch. Cranbourne Atomic

Ch. Cranbourne Arial winning best of breed at West Highland White Terrier Club of America Specialty, 1950, with his owner, Mrs. John T. Marvin, and judge, Mrs. Marian Eppley.

placing at the top. This dog was by Ch. Charan Minstrel ex Eastland's Binny.

Following these came two of the most consistent show winners. They did their winning in overlapping periods which helped bring the breed tremendous acclaim. The first was Mr. Perry Chadwick's Canadian-bred Ch. Highland Ursa Major. This dog commenced his big winning in 1947 when he won best in show at Dayton and Indianapolis. The following year, 1948, he was best dog in show at Jacksonville, Des Moines, Savannah, and Oshkosh, and, in 1949, he topped the Skokie (Chicago area) show, making a total of seven U.S. shows to his credit.

The second was Mrs. John T. Marvin's homebred Ch. Cranbourne Arial, who won his first best in show at Louisville in 1948, coming from the classes to complete his championship. In 1949, he won both at Wheeling and Macomb County (Detroit area), and, in 1950, he captured best at Portland, Indiana. The following year, 1951, a daughter of Arial's, Ch. Klintilloch Molly Dee, an American-bred owned and jointly bred by Mrs. S. M. Blue, turned the trick at Kokomo, Indiana, for the only win that year. Molly Dee was out of Mossbank Nokomis of Thornhill.

1952 brought two best in show awards to the same dog, Mrs. Almary Henderson's Ch. Humby's Dipper. Dipper won his shows at Colorado Springs and Klamath Falls, Oregon. He was Canadian-bred, by Humby's Centaurus ex Highland Antares. Next in line was Ch. Cranbourne Atomic, another of Mrs. Marvin's homebreds and another sired by Ch. Cranbourne Arial. The win was made at Lexington, Kentucky, in 1953. The following year, 1954, Atomic won again at Vincennes, Indiana. Concurrently, Miss Barbara Worcester's English import, Ch. Cruben Dextor, won his first best in show at Brooklyn in 1953 and then won two more in 1954 at Canandaigua, N.Y., and Tonawanda, N.Y. The year 1954 also made a new record with a third Westie winning best in show, and this time it was the third bitch in history. The win was at Enid, Oklahoma, and was made by Robert Lowry's English import, Ch. Shiningcliff Donark

Dancer (English Ch. Shiningcliff Simon ex Donark Determined). 1955 was a lean year for the breed with only one best in show being recorded at Columbus, Ohio, by a new name, Ch. Cravat Coronation (Crawford's Teddy Bear ex Yowel's Honey Girl). An American-bred, Coronation was owned by his breeder, William Worley.

The year 1956 was again a banner year for the breed with five best in show awards. These were made by four different dogs, three of them new to the honor. The first went to the English import Ch. Cruben Flashback (Cruben Faerdale ex Cruben Elsa) at High Point, N.C., and the second to another English dog, Ch. Tulyar of Trenean at Tonawanda, N.Y. Both of these were owned by Miss Barbara Worcester. The third and fourth wins were recorded in rapid succession by another homebred owned by Mrs. John T. Marvin, Ch. Cranbourne Alexandrite, at Mansfield, Ohio, where he came from the classes to best in show, and then at Portland, Indiana, where he again topped the boards scarcely a month after his first triumph. The fifth was scored by Ch. Shiningcliff Donark Dancer at Wichita. It was her second top win.

In 1957, three Highlanders were tops at all-breed shows. Ch. Cruben Flashback repeated his 1956 triumph at High Point, N.C., while another import, Ch. Culbahn Garry won his first best in show at Beaumont, Texas. Garry was owned by B. F. and N. Crawford and was by Eng. Ch. Hasty Bits ex Culbahn Lily. The final show winner for the year was Ch. Wigtown Talent Scout owned by Mrs. B. G. Frame. This homebred triumphed at Hodgenville, Ky. and was by Wigtown Feather Merchant ex Wigtown Notorious. There were no best in show wins in 1958 although several dogs continued to do well in the groups. The following year, however, found Ch. Wigtown Talent Scout coming back to score at St. Louis. He had previously gained high honor by placing best American bred in show at the Chicago International. The dog continued on his winning ways with a third best at Peoria, Ill. in 1960. The same year found Miss Worcester's import, Ch. Symmetra Snip (Symmetra Skirmish ex

84

Ch. Shiningcliff Donark Dancer, a best in show winner and the dam of seven champions. She was handled by Mabel Millichip Lehmann.

Ch. Symmetra Snip with handler, Cliff Hallmark.

Symmetra Serener) winning shows at Fayetteville and Charleston in the Carolinas and topping it off with a best in show at Montgomery County Kennel Club's all-Terrier event, a cherished honor for any Terrier.

Wishing Well Kennels really broke the race wide open in 1961 when Ch. Elfinbrook Simon (Calluna the Laird ex Ichmell Gay Miss) began his record-breaking streak. During the year the dog captured 12 best in shows to completely eclipse all previous records. So startling was this feat that the entire dog world took notice. Nor were they led astray for in early 1962 the dog did what only one other Westie had ever done—he went best in show at Westminster. This event, always considered the top show quality-wise in the nation, is a plum that stamps the winner as "a great one" and always adds glory to the breed. This was the impetus required to start the Highlander rocketing upwards in popularity. A survey of the records will show that 1962 was a turning point in this respect. The steady and rather rapid upswing in popularity since then has been little short of phenomenal and Simon must be given the credit for this impetus. But to complete Simon's record, to prove that his 1961 triumphs were no flash in the pan, the dog duplicated the feat in 1962 with another dozen best in shows climaxed with a triumph at the huge Harbor Cities affair, bringing his lifetime total to 24. One other dog, Ch. Klintilloch Mercator (Ch. Rannoch Dune Defiance ex Rannoch Dune Merrilee) made the grade in 1962. He captured the honor at Colorado Springs for his owners, Robert and Roberta Momberger. This made the count for the year 13, certainly not unlucky for the breed, and indeed a new record high.

Simon was retired in 1962 although he made a comeback with one more ring appearance in 1968 to win the California Specialty, an exceptional feat for "an oldtimer." His retirement left the field devoid of the big winner in 1963 but several dogs came along to take up the challenge. One was Mrs. Fischer's Ch. Wolvey Pickwick (Wolvey Piper's Tune ex Wolvey Padella) who picked up a best in show at Stone City. Another

86

Ch. Cranbourne Alexandrite winning the Group, at Mansfield, 1956, prior to winning the show. Judge, Walter Reeves; handler, Mrs. Marvin.

Ch. Tulyar of Trenean with Henry Sayres.

Ch. Whitebriar Jalisker, sire of Ch. De-Go Hubert, with his handler Michelle Leathers Billings.

was Ch. Whitebriar Journeyman (Famecheck Gay Crusader ex Whitebriar Juana), owned jointly by Mrs. Sayres and Sally Hudson, who topped two events, Whidbey Island and Kansas City, to make the breed's total three for the year. Pickwick repeated his accomplishment the following year at Milwaukee to join Mrs. Carl Furhmann's Ch. Tumbleweed's High Hopes (Tumbleweed's Proud Piper ex Wishing Well's Cotton Candy), who captured the honor at Flint, Mich.

The year 1965 brought out three new winners. Ch. Maxwelton Freshman (Ch. Maxwelton Professor ex Maxwelton Dance Date), owned and bred by Robert Lowry, won at Little Rock, Ark.; R. H. Gustin's Ch. Tamlor's Danny O'Dunoon (Ch. Maxwelton Helpful Henry ex Argyle's Dunoon Damsel), took Salt Lake City from the classes; and Ch. Rannoch Dune Down Beat (Ch. Rannoch Dune Demon ex Rannoch Dune Music), owned by Mrs. B. G. Frame, captured the fall specialty of the parent club over a record entry of 91 and then went on to win best in show at the Indianapolis all-breed event with which the specialty was held. This was the first top win for Down Beat but, as the record will develop, by no means the last.

The year 1966 was not spectacular although Down Beat contined to win well with four more best in shows. He was aided by Mrs. C. C. Fawcett's homebred, Ch. Forest Glen Simon Sez Be Brisk (Ch. Elfinbrook Simon ex Ch. Brisk of Forest Glen) who captured the top award at Columbia, Mo. In 1967 Down Beat won five more shows and a host of groups and brought the breed its first recognition in the "ratings." This occurred when the dog was adjudged "Top Terrier" of the year, an honor that brought substantial publicity to the breed. During the same year, the Herman Fellton's Ch. Whitebriar Jalisker (Whitebriar Jimolo ex Whitebriar Jaffa), who was destined to become an even bigger winner, topped three more events to give the breed a total of eight "bests" for the year.

The breed made a new record in 1968, a record that past events indicate will only be transitory. During the period no less than 25 shows were topped by Highlanders. Leading the

Ch. Forest Glen Simon Sez Be Brisk, best in show winner, owned by Mrs. C. C. Fawcett.

Ch. Tumbleweed's High Hopes.

Ch. Whitebriar Journeyman.

winners' list was Ch. Rannoch Dune Down Beat with eleven and 26 Terrier groups. He was followed closely by Ch. White-briar Jalisker, who won nine shows and 30 Terrier groups. In addition, Mrs. G. F. Church's, Ch. Alpingay Impressario (Warberry Satellite ex Warberry Wide-Awake) claimed two shows, while Mrs. Weaver's, Ch. Ugadale Artist's Model (Ugadale Aristocrat ex Eriegael Winter Witch), Miss Katharine Hayward's homebred, Ch. Huntinghouse Little Fella (Ch. Triskett's Most Happy Fella ex Ch. Huntinghouse Twinklestar), and Dr. Dickie's, Ch. Alderbrook Jolly Roger (Snowcliff Lucky Strike ex Wishing Well's Fancy Frills) captured one apiece.

Nineteen sixty-nine has been another highly successful year for the Westie breed. Ch. Rannoch Dune Down Beat captured four additional best in show awards to bring his lifetime total to 25, thus eclipsing the previous record held by Elfinbrook Simon. In winning his 25th top award, Down Beat also captured his 99th Terrier group, another all-time breed record. It is understood that the dog was retired from competition upon making the record.

Other previous best in show winners mentioned heretofore that have done well since the close of 1968 include Ch. White-briar Jalisker who, although shown sparingly claimed one additional best and Ch. Alpingay Impresario, who has added four more to his excellent record.

During 1969 several other dogs also came into prominence. One of these, Mrs. Jane Henderson's Ch. De-Go Hubert, a son of Jalisker, has done exceedingly well under the guidance of Clifford Hallmark, winning 8 best in shows in strong company. Another newcomer is Wishing Well Kennel's Ch. Birkfell Lyme-hill Solstice who made his title quickly, and under the expert handling of the late Henry Sayres, won four top awards and innumerable groups. Miss Bergit Zakschewski's many-titled Ch. Monsieur Aus Der Flerlage topped two shows in America to add to a total that includes top wins in several other countries. The dog is always owner-handled and conditioned. Ch. D and D's Dead Ringer, owned by Mr. and Mrs. R. L. Hannah is another of the breed to win a top award. This adds to a total of 24 top awards by seven different dogs in 1969.

Ch. Rannoch Dune Down Beat, handled by George Ward, winning the West Highland White Terrier Club of America 1967 Specialty at New York City. Author John T. Marvin is the judge.

Ch. De-Go Hubert, owned by Jane Esther Henderson and bred by Dean Hughes, was one of the mightiest winners in the history of the breed. He was handled by Clifford Hallmark to many top awards in the course of his stellar career.

Am. and Can. Ch. Alderbrook Jolly Roger, C.D., best in show winner, owned by Dr. Lois Dickie.

Int. Ch. Monsieur aus der Flerlage, best in show winner, owned by Bergit Coady.

The year 1970 found Mrs. Henderson's, Ch. De-Go Hubert (Ch. Whitebriar Jalisker ex Whitebriar Jetstar) rewriting the book with a total of 16 best in show awards to add to his mounting record. Chs. Alpingay Impressario and Lymehills Birkfell Solstice each added one more to their totals while a newcomer, Mrs. Frame's Ch. Purston Pinmoney Pedlar (Pillerton Peterman ex Pinmoney Pride) entered the lists with six top awards. The following year (1971), both Hubert and Pedlar captured six each while Dr. and Mrs. G. G. Meisels' Ch. White Oaks Lover Boy added a singleton with their eight-year-old daughter, Laura, showing the dog. Nineteen-seventy-two found "the Pedlar dog" picking up 13 more bests while three new competitors entered the charmed circle. They were, Allan and Marlene Kotlisky's Ch. Wiloglen's Willoughboy (Ch. Waideshouse Wiloughby ex Ch. Rudh'Re Jillet) with two and Mrs. Constance Jones' Ch. Pillerton Peterkin (Pillerton Peterman ex Pillerton Polka) and Mrs. Keenan's and Mrs. Schiele's jointly owned newcomer Ch. Pinmoney Puck (Pillerton Peterman ex Trudy's Delight), and a great little showman, claiming a single award each.

In 1973, four Highlanders broke all previous records for the breed with a total of 33 best in show awards. Heading the list was Pedlar with 20 top triumphs followed by Puck with seven, Dr. A. T. Hunt's newcomer, Ch. Highland's Angus (Pillerton Perry ex Pinmoney Portia), four and Ch. Braidholme White Tornado of Binate (Lucky of Loughore ex Braidholme White Lady) owned by Mr. Kate Seeman, one. The same year found Mrs. Jones' Ch. Purston Polly Perkins (Pillerton Peterman ex Birkfell Screech Owl) becoming only the fourth bitch in history to capture a best in show award in the U.S. Pedlar's accomplishments in 1973 were sufficiently impressive to carry him to top Terrier of the year in several national polls. In 1974 another new dog came upon the scene. This was Dr. A. T. Hunt's imported Ch. Ardenrun 'Andsome of Purston (Whitebriar Jonfair ex Ardenrun Agitator) who was exhibited for only a portion of the year but nonetheless captured nine top placements. He was followed by Ch. Braid-

93

holme White Tornado of Binate who added eight to his impressive total, Ch. Purston Pinmoney Pedlar, still a factor at the shows, with five, the previously mentioned Ch. Highland's Angus, two and Ch. Pinmoney Puck one. A newcomer to the best in show circle, Ch. Keithall Pilot, owned by Mrs. Joanne Glodek and shown by her daughter Jaimi, took top honors in Puerto Rico to bring the year's total to 26 bests in show for the breed.

The year 1975 became a period of retrenchment for the breed. Ch. Ardenrun 'Andsome of Purston continued his dominance with 19 more top awards and only one other Highlander helped the year's total. This was a newcomer, imported Ch. Commander of Tintibar (Checkbar Donsie Kythe ex Sally of Clyndarose), owned by Mrs. Jones, who captured a singleton together with many group triumphs. A strong winner that joined the "best in show club" during 1976 was Bobbe and Jerry London's Ch. London's Duffy MacDuff. Many times a group and specialty winner, "Duffy" scored his first best at Corn Belt KC in May and has added at least one other top prize as this goes to press. Finally Mrs. Anita Becky's Ch. B-J's Sir Becket (Ch. Ardenrun 'Andsome of Purston ex Ch. Arnholme Dove) entered the best in show circle in 1976 with a top award at the Southern Colorado KC.

Several others have done well in the groups but have been unable to crack the barrier of best in show. This brings the record up-to-date and demonstrates that the Highlander has advanced tremendously during the past fifteen years. Best in show awards are not unusual today and the breed representative is usually a much-feared group competitor. Truly, the West Highland White Terrier has now become established as a quality member of the Terrier tribe. Further, if the breed continues on its present course of improvement, the future will be even more fruitful.

Ch. Lymehills Birkfell Solstice, owned by Wishing Well Kennels, was owner-handled to best of breed at the 1970 national specialty under John W. Hillman.

Ch. Purston Pinmoney Pedlar, owned by the late Mrs. B. G. Frame and bred by the Rev. Michael Collings, is the top best in show Westie in history. He was handled by George Ward to his glittering record.

Ch. Pinmoney Puck, owned by Wishing Well Kennels and Marjadele Schiele, was the winner of numerous important awards.

Ch. Pillerton Peterkin, owned by Constance C. Jones and bred by Sylvia J. Kearsey.

Ch. Purston Polly Perkins, owned by Constance C. Jones and bred by Rev. Collings, was a 1973 best in show winner—the first Westie bitch in many years to take a top award.

Ch. Commander of Tintibar, owned by Constance C. Jones and bred by Mrs. E. Brittain.

Ch. White Oaks Lover Boy, owned by Dr. and Mrs. G. G. Meisels, was piloted to a best in show at the Calcasieu (Louisiana) show by the owners' eight-year-old daughter, Laura. The win made Laura Meisels the youngest best in show handler in the history of dog showing.

Ch. Braidholme White Tornado of Binate, owned by Mr. and Mrs. George Seeman and bred in Ireland by J. Morrow put together a string of stunning victories during his campaign. He was best of breed at the specialty in 1973 from the classes and repeated in 1974 going on to best in show at Montgomery County.

Ch. London's Duffy Mac Duf, owned by Bobbe and Jerry London and bred by Joyce R. Lempke, is a multiple best in show and specialty winner.

Ch. Ardenrun Andsome of Purston, owned by Alvaro T. Hunt, M.D. has enjoyed a brilliant career in the American show ring. Imported in 1974, he was a group winner before completing his championship and numbers among his abundant victories the terrier group at Westminster in 1975 and best in show at the 1976 edition of the Montgomery County all-terrier classic.

Ch. Keithall Pilot, owned by Joanne and Joseph Glodek, was handled to a best in show in Puerto Rico by the Glodeks' 12-year-old daughter, Jaimi.

Ch. Highlands Angus, owned by Alvaro T. Hunt, M.D. and bred by Mrs. M. A. Madden, was a strong winner under specialist and all-breed judges alike.

Can. Ch. Rowmore Ardifuir, owned by Mr. and Mrs. Victor Blochin and the first of the breed to win a Terrier Group in Canada.

The Westie in Canada

Canadian activity in the breed, while not keeping pace with the growth of interest in the U.S. initially, has been increasing dramatically during the past ten years or so. Canadian-owned dogs are now taking their place among the top-quality animals to be seen at any show and offer a useful cross section of English imports and Canadian-bred specimens. In the immediate postwar era, much of the glory at Canadian events was claimed by American-owned West Highlands. These were taken above the border to compete for their Canadian titles. Such dogs as Chs. Highland Ursa Major (Canadian-bred but American-owned), Cruben Dextor, Edgerstoune Valley Belle, Cruben Melphis Chloe, Elfinbrook Simon, Alpingay Impressario, Rannoch-Dune Down Beat and more lately, Kristajen Cracker-jack, Purston Pinmoney Pedlar and Famecheck Busy Body are just a few who made news and Canadian titles. Of course, there were a number of Canadian exhibits that did well too in the overall competition. Among these were, Chs. Shiningcliff Sprig, Bencruachan Punch, Pixiewood Pip, Rose-

Can. Ch. Highland Castor, C.D., bred
and owned by Edith Humby.

Ch. Bencruachan Proteus, bred by Victor and Mrs. Blochin and owned by
Louise R. Lang.

neath White Knight, Dina-Ken's Little Pip, both of the last good winners in the U.S. too, Highland Arcturus (later American-owned) and Whitebriar Journeyman to name a few.

Before moving on to more recent fanciers and events, some well-deserved tributes must be given to two efforts, both begun well before the war, that did much to keep the breed in the eye of the Canadian public for many years. These are the Bencruachan establishment of Victor and the late Mrs. Blochin and the Highland Kennels of the late Rosamond Billett and Miss Edith Humby. Bencruachan has long been a bulwark of the breed and made a name many years ago through the exploits of Ch. Rowmore Ardifuir which was maintained by the likes of Bencruachan Champagne, Proteus and Hope and in more recent times by Cruben Dugald, a litter brother to Ch. Cruben Moray of Clairedale and the sire of such worthies as Chs. Roseneath White Knight and Roseneath Commander, etc. Unfortunately, Dugald died at an early age and surely before he had attained his full potential. Victor Blochin is still vitally interested in the breed but has curtailed his activities drastically. The Highland Kennels of Miss Billett have been carried on and very ably by Miss Humby for many years, although the prefix has been changed. The greatest offering to the fancy from this establishment was unquestionably, Ch. Highland Ursa Major followed by the good winner, Ch. Humby's Dipper. Again, this kennel has offered a steady output of quality dogs and has helped the growth of the breed thereby.

Some 25 years ago, Mr. and Mrs. J. Neill Malcolm were strong supporters of the breed and Mr. Malcolm has the distinct honor of being a direct descendant of Col. E. D. Malcolm. Unfortunately, while interest still exists, the kennels are closed. Another very active effort begun after the war is the 'of the Rouge suffix seen frequently above and below the border. Unfortunately Mr. Daniell-Jenkins was killed in an automobile accident in 1960 but Mrs. Daniell-Jenkins has carried on helped by her daugher, Mrs. Keith Balsdon, who now has her own kennel identified by the prefix Winde Mere. Her homebred, Ch. Winde Mere Gay Gordon has been a consistent winner with a record that includes two best in show awards.

Some of Mrs. Daniell-Jenkins' toppers included the good winner, Ch. Shiningcliff Sprig and more lately, Chs. Danny Boy of the Rouge and Shipmate's Hannibal. Mrs. Daniell-Jenkins still maintains her kennel while fulfilling a demanding schedule of judging both in Canada and the U.S. Mr. and Mrs. T. Adams have also been active for many years and began their effort in the Toronto area and then moved to British Columbia in 1974 where they continue their program. Their fine homebred Ch. Roseneath White Knight is believed to be the first Canadian-bred West Highlander to capture best of breed at the U.S. national Specialty show, an honor he gained from the classes in 1957 and repeated as a special in 1959. The Adams have bred and/or owned many fine dogs in the breed and today have two homebreds, Chs. Feolin Angus of Roseneath and Roseneath Candy Man who have both gained the honor of a best in show triumph. In 1961, the Albert Kayes' (Dreamland) came to the U.S. specialty with their Dina-Ken's Little Pip and claimed best of breed, again from the classes, to repeat the Adams' triumphs. This bitch did some excellent winning above and below the border. Albert Kaye died in 1971 but Mrs. Kaye has continued the effort with great success. To date, Chs. Dreamland's Go-Go Girl, Dreamland's Councillor and Nor'Westie's Wee Roderick have been campaigned to best in show awards, the first two being homebreds.

A host of other Canadians deserve mention for their sterling efforts to breed top Highlanders. Among them are Mrs. Margaret Freemantle of Victoria, B.C. whose Remasais prefix did so well a few years ago, also Fred Fraser who has been active for a number of years with good success. His latest big winner is an English import, Ch. Limehills Special Edition of Lindenhall who has some eighteen best in show awards to date. Mrs. Sally Bremner (formerly Hudson) is another who has enjoyed long and substantial success in the breed. She was the co-owner with Mrs. Sayres of the good winner, Ch. Whitebriar Journeyman who did well on both sides of the border and also owns two other Canadian best in show winners in Chs. Broadridge Bearer and Whitebriar Juryman. Mrs. Bremner is located in British Columbia but shows across the

Ch. Danny Boy of the Rouge, owned by Donna and Karen Peckan.

Ch. Winde Mere Gay Gordon, a best in show winner, owned by
Mrs. Keith Baldson and Mrs. J. H. Daniell-Jenkins and bred by
Mrs. Baldson.

Dominion. Her prefix has always been Sallydean. Strong exhibitors at many Canadian shows in the past were Paul and Margaret McAndrew whose Nor'Westie prefix is seen frequently. Their effort began from an Alaskan base and with excellent success. Their homebred, Ch. Nor'Westie's Wee Piper was exhibited at both American and Canadian shows and has the honor of capturing best in show five times at the Yukon Kennel Club fixture, some sort of a record, to be sure. The McAndrews are now located in California so that Nor'Westie dogs will be seen more often. Two other kennels have had the honor of winning best in show awards in Canada during the past few years. These are Mr. and Mrs. J. F. Crowe's Benbulben Kennels located in Ontario, with two dogs that accomplished the feat, Ch. Whitebriar Jayman and Ch. Headwood Braw Laddie and Miss Lisa Ewles, the fortunate owner, of a double winner in Ch. Roseneath Maxwell Smart. The dog has also done good group placing for his young owner. Surely, this list which is hoped to be complete, shows that Canadian dogs are doing very well at shows above the border. Truly, the West Highlander has come of age and is now a much feared competitor under the maple leaf. Not all exhibitors have had the good fortune to place their dog at the top. Nevertheless this large segment of the fancy is probably the backbone of competition and many excellent specimens are among the competitors—specimens just waiting for the opportunity to move forward. Among this group are, Leonard Hunter (Laurie's) who has been breeding for over a decade. During this time he has bred some five titleholders including Ch. Laurie's Piper of the Rouge, an excellent sire with a dozen or so champions to date for his present owner, Mrs. Daniell-Jenkins; Mr. and Mrs. A. M. McGillivray (Clochnaben) are actively establishing their own bloodlines from Manderley (H. T. Flanagan) and Dreamland (Kaye) stock; Mr. and Mrs. Gary Gray from Calgary with a good homebred bitch in Ch. Cavernmoor Morning Marsh Mist. Ian Petrie (Victoria) is relatively new to the breed, but is the grandson of Fred Dodsworth, one of the earliest Canadian Westie fanciers. Mr. Petrie has reclaimed Dodsworth's original kennel prefix, "Craigside"; Mr. and Mrs. Lorne Gignac of Ottawa, whose Cromarty prefix is

106

Ch. Roseneath Fair Charmer, a group winner, bred, owned and handled by T. S. Adams.

Ch. Roseneath Candy Man, a best in show winner, bred, owned and handled by T. S. Adams.

Ch. Whitebriar Juryman, owned and handled by Sally Bremner, has been fearlessly shown in Canada and is a noted best in show winner in that country.

"C'mon Mike, lemme give ya a kiss." Ch. Whitebriar Jade with young Michael Hudson.

Ch. Broadbridge Bearer,
owned by Sally Bremner, a
best in show winner.

Ch. Sallydean's Macgregor
Wee Rob, owned and bred
by Sally Bremner.

Ch. Laird of the Loch,
owned by Dr. and Mrs.
W. Young and bred by Sally
Bremner.

becoming well-known, have had substantial success. The Gignac children do most of the handling. Other familiar names in the Canadian Fancy include Mrs. Joan Carter (Westvales), Mrs. Pat Cook (Avalen), Mrs. H. T. Flanagan (Manderley) who has been relatively inactive recently, Mr. and Mrs. Ł. S. Frame (O'the Loch), Mr. and Mrs. Joseph Liberman (Jokar's), Gary and Diana Thubron (Shagle), James Scott (Macmer), Mrs. L. J. Sherman (Harridale). One more should be mentioned, for while living in the U.S. she is a Canadian who has been at it for many years. Mrs. Joan Zwicker (Zwicker's) owned a grandson of Ch. Rowemore Ardifuir and also an English import as foundation stock. She is now establishing her own line and exhibits actively in both the U.S. and Canada. It is apparent from the comments heretofore, that Canadians are avid exhibitors and have substantial strength of numbers within the breed fancy. Most exhibit both in the U.S. and Canada and today, one finds the Canadian shows well supported in the breed which guarantees further growth both in numbers and in quality. I might add that competition is strong at most Canadian events since many Americans add their weight to that of the Canadians in an effort to make dual titleholders.

Eng., Can., and Am. Ch.
Shiningcliff Sprig

Dina-Ken's Little Pip.

110

Ch. Nor'Westie's Wee Roderick, leased to Mrs. Kaye by Mrs. McAndrews, became a multiple group and best in show winner in Canada.

Ch. Nor'Westie's Wee Piper, owned by Mrs. McAndrews, is a homebred best in show winner.

Mr. and Mrs. Lorne Gignac's best in show brace Ch. Dancer's Eminence of the Rouge and Denisette Mandan of the Rouge are shown here in a Bermuda win under Louis Murr. This owner-handled pair was twice best brace in show and best terrier brace at International 1972.

Eng. Ch. Wolvey Poster, who can be traced back directly
through the sire's side to Patrician

Eng. Ch. Wolvey Pintail, considered by Mrs. Pacey as one of the best.

Bloodlines of the West Highland White Terrier

As mentioned in previous chapters, the background of the West Highland White was not too accurately chronicled before the beginning of the twentieth century. After this, and specifically from about 1907, the pedigrees of various dogs can be traced with comparative accuracy, and the influence of certain dogs upon the destinies of the breed may be determined.

The first traceable blood of the Westie goes back to a dog named Conas, the fountainhead of the breed. Conas sired five important sons and daughters among a host of others. His famous daughters were Ch. Runag, famous for her great ring success, and Cabaig, equally famous for her producing ability. Cabaig, when bred to a dog named Saighdear, brought forth Brogach, who, when bred to his daughter Culaig, sired the great Ch. Morven. In addition to siring Morven, Brogach fathered Carnoch, who was the sire of Ch. Kiltie, who sired Ch. Rumpus of Glenmere.

Ch. Morven, the first Westie to gain the title, was the sire of many fine dogs such as Ch. Cromar Snowflake, Ch. Cairn Nevis

Ch. Wolvey Patrician, owned and bred by Mrs. C. C. Pacey, whelped September 6, 1924.

```
                                        White Don          Ch. Highclere Rhalet
                    White Laird                            Lady in White
                                        Greenside Tossy    Nevisaig
    Ch. Wolvey Guy                                         Moggill
                                        White Don          Ch. Highclere Rhalet
                    Ch. White Sylph                        Lady in White
                                        White Belle        White Jock
CH. WOLVEY PATRICIAN                                       White Daisy
                                        Ornsay Challenger  Ornsay Stamp
                    Ornsay Bobs                            Ornsay Folly
                                        Crown Princess     Majestic
    Ch. Wolvey Clover                                      Snechda
                                        Barlae Defender    Barlae Snowboy
                    Hedderwick Lass                        Barlae Calliag
                                        Gateside Dolly     Hailes Hector
                                                           Gateside White Gem
```

Ch. Ray of Rushmoor (782014), owned by Mrs. John G. Winant and bred by Miss V. M. Smith-Wood, whelped June 3, 1927.

```
                                        White Laird        White Don
                    Ch. Wolvey Guy                         Greenside Tossy
                                        Ch. White Sylph    White Don
    Ch. Wolvey Patrician                                   White Belle
                                        Ornsay Bobs        Ornsay Challenger
                    Ch. Wolvey Clover                      Crown Princess
                                        Hedderwick Lass    Barlae Defender
CH. RAY OF RUSHMOOR                                        Gateside Dolly
                                        Ch. Highclere Rhalet  Ch. Moresco
                    Ch. Gwern Wilfrid                      Highclere Rival
                                        Wrexham Angela     Wrexham Tomboy
    Binny of Rushmoor                                      Wrexham Lucia
                                        Ch. Chum of Child- Charger of Childwick
                    Noreen                          wick   Grip
                                        Shireen            White Don
                                                           Moccassin Lassie
```

(sire of Lothian Lad, who, in turn, sired Ch. Highclere Roamer), and Lothian Pride, who was the sire of Barlae Perfection. Morven was also the sire of Atholl, said to be his best son.* Atholl had the misfortune of being off-white and his stud services were little in demand. In spite of this, he produced Ch. Glenmhor Model, Ch. Pure Gem, and Lothian Marvel, all widely known and highly useful to the breed.

Going back to the important sons of Conas, we find that when he was bred to Jean, the offspring was Ch. Oronsay, who sired, among others, Ch. Cawston Garry. Another Conas son was Balloch Bhan, who sired Inverailort Roy and Ch. Baughfell's Talisker. The latter was a winner at the Garden in 1910. The third famous son was Dunollie Admiral, who was out of Culaig the dam of the aforementioned Ch. Morven.

Dunollie Admiral was the sire of Chief of Childwick (who headed a strain including Oronsay Snowman and Ch. Morova, who sired Ch. Moresco, the sire of Ch. Highclere Romp) and Ch. Highclere Rhalet, who was out of Highclere Rival. Rhalet blood flowed in the veins of many widely known dogs, including among others, Ch. Highclere Rescuer; Bacchus of the Creek, great-grandsire of Ch. Placemore Caution; Harviestoun Rhalet, sire of Crivoch Cadet; Ch. Gwern Wilfrid, sire of Ch. Wolvey Wish; and White Don.

White Don sired the great bitch Ch. White Sylph and is also responsible for many sons who proved to be dynamic influences on the breed. Most important of these were White Demon, sire of Ch. White Smasher; Puck of Dane's End, sire of Ch. Moses of Dane's End (the sire of Ch. Ophir's Rowdy) ; Maulden Scout, sire of William Under the Steeple and White Laird. White Laird, when bred to his half sister Ch. White Sylph, produced Ch. Wolvey Guy, who gained undying fame as the sire of Ch. Wolvey Patrician, patriarch of the "modern" blood.

Ch. Wolvey Patrician was probably the greatest single influence on the background of our breed. He was not only a great show dog but also his blood dominates the breed today

* *The West Highland White Terrier,* by Holland Buckley, 1911

115

Ch. Wolvey Poacher, owned and bred by Mrs. C. C. Pacey, whelped December 16, 1931.

```
                                   Ch. Wolvey Patrician Ch. Wolvey Guy
                          Clint Crofter                 Ch. Wolvey Clover
                                   Clint Sapper         White Don
         Ch. Wolvey Pepper                              Clint Chaste
                                   Rufus Under the      William Under the Steeple
                          Pixie of Shel-   Steeple      Girdee Under the Steeple
                              wyn    Winchmore Bunty     Placemore Trifle
CH. WOLVEY POACHER                                      Springrove Snow
                                   Ch. Wolvey Guy       White Laird
                          Ch. Wolvey Patrician          Ch. White Sylph
                                   Ch. Wolvey Clover    Ornsay Bobs
         Wolvey Petal                                   Hedderwick Lass
                                   Ch. White Smasher    White Demon
                          Wolvey Patience               Greenside Tossy
                                   Ch. Wolvey Clover    Ornsay Bobs
                                                        Hedderwick Lass
```

Ch. Edgerstoune Radium (A299575), owned and bred by Mrs. John G. Winant, whelped October 15, 1938.

```
                                   Ch. Wolvey Patrician Ch. Wolvey Guy
                          Ch. Ray of Rushmoor           Ch. Wolvey Clover
                                   Binny of Rushmoor    Ch. Gwern Wilfrid
         Ch. Edgerstoune Roughy                         Noreen
                                   Ch. Clint Cocktail   Clint Crofter
                          Ch. Clint Casserole           Medusa of the Creek
                                   Clint Caltha         Positive Under the Steeple
CH. EDGERSTOUNE RADIUM                                  Thistle Under the Steeple
                                   Ch. Edgerstoune      Ch. Ray of Rushmoor
                          Ch. Edgerstoune   Rastus      Ch. Clint Casserole
                              Wallie   Edgerstoune Remus Clint Courtier
         Edgerstoune Raith                              Ch. Clint Casserole
                                   Clint Courtier       Wolvey Patron
                          Ch. Edgerstoune Rhea          Eriska Bhan
                                   Ch. Clint Casserole  Ch. Clint Cocktail
                                                        Clint Caltha
```

Ch. Wolvey Pattern of Edgerstoune (A290740), owned by Mrs. John G. Winant and bred by Mrs. C. C. Pacey, whelped April 20, 1937.

```
                                   Ch. Wolvey Pepper    Clint Crofter
                          Wolvey Peacock                Pixie of Shelwyn
                                   Scuttle of the Roe    Skelum of the Roe
         Ch. Wolvey Prefect                             Peek-a-Boo of the Roe
                                   Ch. Wolvey Pickle    Ch. Dornie Busybody
                          Wolvey Popinjay               Wolvey Patience
                                   Ch. Wolvey Pauline   Ch. Wolvey Patrician
CH. WOLVEY PATTERN OF EDGERSTOUNE                       Ch. White Sylvia
                                   Wolvey Pepper        Clint Crofter
                          Ch. Wolvey Poacher            Pixie of the Roe
                                   Wolvey Petal         Ch. Wolvey Patrician
         Ch. Wolvey Privet of Edgerstoune               Wolvey Patience
                                   Raymond of Rushmoor  Clint Crofter
                          Rosalie of Rushmoor           Binny of Rushmoor
                                   Ruby of Rushmoor     Roderick of Rushmoor
                                                        Ruth of Rushmoor
```

through the descendants of his son English and American Ch. Ray of Rushmoor and his grandson English Ch. Wolvey Poacher. Patrician was whelped on September 6, 1924, and was bred by Mrs. C. Pacey. Close study of his pedigree will show a strong infusion of the Conas line. Since this book is basically directed to breed efforts in the United States, no attempt will be made to delve further into the bloodlines of other countries. Suffice it to say that Ray of Rushmoor surely did his part in this country to make the Highlander what he is today. Ray's most famous offspring include ten champions, nine of which bore the Edgerstoune prefix. These were Ch. Edgerstoune Rastus, Ch. Edgerstoune Rebel, Ch. Edgerstoune Ravenna, Ch. Edgerstoune Royal, Ch. Edgerstoune Roxie, Ch. Edgerstoune Roughy, the litter mates Chs. Edgerstoune Requa, Edgerstoune Ringlet, and Edgerstoune Rowdy, and, last but by no means least, Ch. Robinridge MacBeth. Several of these carried on as producers. Ch. Robinridge MacBeth sired Ch. Belmertle Alba, Ch. Robinridge Bubbles, and Ch. Robinridge Bimelick, C.D.X. MacBeth also sired Canadian Ch. Belmertle Aldrich, who had three U.S. champion offspring in Highland Sagittarius, Highland Venus, and Highland Ursa Major. The last did extremely well and was responsible for Ch. Inverary Emperor, Ch. Cranbourne Alice, Ch. Wigtown Countess, and the littermates Ch. Heather-Tyke's Olivia, Ch. Heather-Tyke's Ochone, and Ch. Heather-Tyke's Orlando. Ch. Highland Ursa Major also sired Ch. Heather-Tyke's Duncan, who sired Ch. Seventh Heaven's Lady in White and Ch. Highland Pollux's Thistle Bud. Ch. Edgerstoune Roughy, who was another Ray son, proved to be a strong sire with six champions to his credit, including Ch. Edgerstoune Radium (in his own right a great sire), together with Ch. Robinridge Commodore, Ch. Robinridge Miracle, Ch. Robinridge Siren, Ch. Robinridge Countess, and Ch. Robinridge Cherie.

Ch. Edgerstoune Radium's influence is still felt in the breed, since many of his progeny are living and are still producing. In all, eight champion sons and daughters represent this great dog.

117

These include Ch. Cranbourne Agatha (the last puppy he sired), Ch. Edgerstoune Ripple, Ch. Edgerstoune Netta, Ch. Heather of the Orchard, Ch. Highland Laddie, Ch. Edgerstoune Cindy, C.D., Ch. Billikin, and Ch. Battison Beacon, who was his most famous son. Beacon, in turn, sired Ch. Mi Evening Lad, C.D.; Ch. Mi Mon, C.D.; Ch. Paisley Hill Hathor; Ch. Mi Mheall Beacon; Ch. Yowell's Little Bit of Sugar; Ch. Klintilloch Radiance; and Ch. Cranbourne Angus, who was the sire of Ch. Cranbourne Annabelle, Ch. Cranbourne Alexandrite, and Ch. Cranbourne Arial. Arial, in turn, sired Ch. Klintilloch Molly Dee, Ch. Cranbourne Atomic, Ch. Cranbourne Angie, Ch. Cranbourne Alvina, Ch. Nairnshire Sugar Cookie, and Ch. Nairnshire Dandy.

Two more of Beacon's sons have done well at stud: Ch. Mi Mon, C.D., has sired Ch. Squire of Parkwoods, Ch. Wigtown Deborah, and Ch. Mi Frances; while Ch. Highland Laddie sired Ch. Caledonia's Will O' the Wisp and Ch. Angus of Casterbridge. It is clear that the influence of Radium is strong and that only the years to come will tell the full story, for many of his descendants are still in their prime.

Turning now to the other branch of the Patrician line, we find that Wolvey Patrician was the sire of Wolvey Petal, the dam of English Ch. Wolvey Poacher, and was also Poacher's great-grandsire on the paternal side. Poacher established a strong following in the United States through many imports that carried his direct blood in their veins. Among his sons and daughters were Ch. Edgerstoune Raoul, Ch. Edgerstoune Rohays, Ch. Heather Hill David, Ch. Heather Hill Nora, Ch. Wolvey Privet of Edgerstoune, Ch. Heather Hill Patrick, Ch. Wolvey Prophet of Edgerstoune, Ch. Wolvey Poet of Charan, and Wolvey Phantom of Edgerstoune. Wolvey Phantom sired Ch. Edgerstoune Rightful and Ch. Edgerstoune Royalty, who, in turn, was the sire of Ch. Edgerstoune Starlet. Ch. Heather Hill Patrick sired Ch. Heather Hill Peacock and Ch. Heather Hill Rita, while Ch. Heather Hill David sired Ch. Heather Hill Partridge, a stud force with five champions to his credit,

Ch. Cranbourne Arial (R11183), owned and bred by Mrs. John T. Marvin, whelped November 10, 1946.

		Ch. Edgerstoune Radium	Ch. Edgerstoune Roughy
	Ch. Battison Beacon		Edgerstoune Raith
		Edgerstoune Evening	Ch. Edgerstoune Rastus
Ch. Cranbourne Angus		Lassie	Ch. Edgerstoune Roxie
	Springmeade Tam O'Shan-		Blashford Benedict
	Cranbourne Mi Paisley	ter	Battison Bess
		Ch. Rothmore's Mheall	Ch. Mheall Dirk
CH. CRANBOURNE ARIAL		Dhu	Rothmore's Betty
		Ch. Heather Hill David	Ch. Wolvey Poacher
	Ch. Heather Hill Partridge		Wolvey Picture
		Heather Hill Pinfeather	Ch. Heather Hill Patrick
Ch. Cranbourne Amanda			Leal Rhua
		Ch. Battison Beacon	Ch. Edgerstoune Radium
	Ch. Mi Mheall Beacon		Edgerstoune Evening Lassie
		Rothmore's Mheall Dun-	Ch. Mheall Dirk
		ollie	Sally Lunn O'Petriburg

Ch. Cruben Dextor (center) with his sons, the littermates Cruben Dugald (left) and Cruben Moray at ten months of age.

namely, Ch. Rothmore's Hamish, Ch. Crawford's Lucky Penny, Ch. Crawford's Powder Puff, Ch. Cranbourne Amanda, and Ch. Paisley Hill Hailfellow.

Ch. Wolvey Poet of Charan's most widely known son was Ch. Charan Minstrel, who was responsible for Ch. Shirley Bliss of Belmertle, Ch. Belmertle Imogene, Ch. Belmertle Vanity, Ch. Belmertle Utopia, Ch. Belmertle Zephyr, and Ch. Gillette's Lord Tuffington (the sire of Ch. Cynbaren Adventuress, Ch. Glencaven's Janie, Ch. Mi Tuffette of Parkwoods, Ch. Glencaven's Snowball, and Ch. Camelhill Mr. Tuffy). Ch. Camelhill Mr. Tuffy sired Ch. Blak-N-Wite Warspite, Ch. Blak-N-Wite Waveta, Ch. Blak-N-Wite Victor, Ch. Blak-N-Wite Wistella, C.D., and Ch. Blak-N-Wite Veta. Zephyr sired three champions in Ch. Wee Winnie of Bonniebelle, Ch. Heatherbelle Essential Ian, and Ch. Heatherbelle Miss Muffet.

Some dogs that remained in England require mention since they did a great deal for the breed in this country. English Ch. Shiningcliff Simon was one of these, for he sired Ch. Tyndrum Simonetta, Ch. Shiningcliff Sim, Ch. Shiningcliff Sprig, Ch. Shiningcliff Snowflake, and Ch. Shiningcliff Donark Dancer, among others that did well here. Another was Eng. Ch. Hookwood Mentor, the sire of Ch. Cruben Dextor, Ch. Scoram Jinty of Clairedale, Ch. Brisk of Branston of Edgertoune, Ch. Culbahn White Ribbon of Robinridge, Ch. Hookwood Smartie of Clairedale, and Ch. Hookwood Marquis. Still a third was Cruben Flash, who bears mention because he sired (1) Ch. Cruben Melphis Chloe, a great show bitch and the dam of Cruben Dextor and (2) Ch. Cruben Cranny of Edgerstoune, who did well both in the ring and at stud in this country. Cranny's champion offspring were Cruben Victory, Inverary Charlemagne, Rannoch's Lilliput, Inverary Firebrand, and Edgerstoune Valley Belle, another great show bitch.

Returning to Ch. Cruben Dextor, who won titles in England, Canada and the United States, there is no doubt that he was one of the outstanding stud dogs of all times. One would expect great things from a dog so royally bred (Eng. Ch. Hookwood

120

Ch. Shiningcliff Simon, owned and bred by Mrs. J. Finch, whelped May 10, 1945.

CH. SHININGCLIFF SIMON

Ch. Leal Flurry	Ch. Calluna Ruairidh	Ch. Ray of Rushmoor	Ch. Wolvey Patrician
			Binny of Rushmoor
		Calluna Cranreuch	Ch. Ophir Chiel
			Cooden Security
	My Riviera Rose	Ch. Skelum of the Roe	Highclere Resolute
			Shiela
		Peek-a-Boo of the Roe	Harvieston Rhalet
			White Heather of the Port
Walney Thistle	Ch. Wolvey Prefect	Ch. Wolvey Peacock	Ch. Wolvey Pepper
			Scuttle of the Roe
		Wolvey Popinjay	Wolvey Pickle
			Ch. Wolvey Pauline
	White Sheen of Wick	Dougald	Mheall Slogan
			Mheall Churran
		Cora	Calluna Ardrishaig
			Mheall Spur

Ch. Highland Ursa Major (R21957), owned by Perry Chadwick and bred by Miss Rosamond Billett, whelped August 26, 1945.

CH. HIGHLAND URSA MAJOR

Belmertle Aldrich	Ch. Robinridge MacBeth	Ch. Ray of Rushmoor	Ch. Wolvey Patrician
			Binny of Rushmoor
		Edgerstoune Rarity	Clint Courtier
			Clint Creena of Edgerstoune
	Ch. Robinridge Cherie	Ch. Edgerstoune Roughy	Ch. Ray of Rushmoor
			Ch. Clint Casserole
		Ch. Wolvey Pace of Edgerstoune	Ch. Wolvey Patrician
			Wolvey Promise
Edgerstoune Stardust	Ch. Edgerstoune Roughy	Ch. Ray of Rushmoor	Ch. Wolvey Patrician
			Binny of Rushmoor
		Ch. Clint Casserole	Ch. Clint Cocktail
			Clint Caltha
	Ch. Edgerstoune Starlet	Ch. Edgerstoune Royalty	Wolvey Phantom of Edgerstoune
			Edgerstoune Raith
		Edgerstoune Joyce	Ch. Wolvey Prophet of Edgerstoune
			Ch. Clint Casserole

Ch. Hookwood Mentor, owned by Miss
E. E. Wade and bred by A. Brown,
whelped May 14, 1947.

```
                                                              Ch. Wolvey Peacock
                                      Ch. Wolvey Prefect      Wolvey Popinjay
                    Furzefield Provider                       Furzefield Prosper
                                      Ch. Placemore Pros-     Flinders Molly
         Furzefield Piper                         perity      Ch. Leal Flurry
                                      Ch. Melbourne Math-     Leal Chieftainess
                    Furzefield Penelope           ais        Furzefield Provider
                                      Furzefield Prunella     Furzefield Print
CH. HOOKWOOD MENTOR                                           Ch. Wolvey Poacher
                                      Ch. Wolvey Prophet      Rosalie of Rushmoor
                    Brantvale Blinker                         Mheall Firkin
                                      Belenoch                Colleen of the Roe
         Bonchurch Bunty                                      Furzefield Provider
                                      Bonchurch Barman        Furzefield Print
                    Bonchurch Babs                            Furzefield Periwig
                                      Furzefield Partisan     Lizzette
```

Ch. Cruben Dextor (R106142), owned
by Wishing Well Kennels and bred
by Dr. and Mrs. A. Russell, whelped
January 17, 1950.

```
                                      Furzefield Provider     Ch. Wolvey Prefect
                    Furzefield Piper                          Ch. Placemore Prosperity
                                      Furzefield Penelope     Ch. Melbourne Mathias
         Ch. Hookwood Mentor                                  Furzefield Prunella
                                      Brantvale Blinker       Ch. Wolvey Prophet of Edgerst
                    Bonchurch Bunty                           Belenoch
                                      Bonchurch Babs          Bonchurch Barman
CH. CRUBEN DEXTOR                                             Furzefield Partisan
                                      Eoghan Ban              Wolvey Pippin
                    Cruben Flash                              Calluna Bimm
                                      Cruben Flame            Cruben Stalwart
         Ch. Cruben Melphis Chloe                             Mhairi Bhan
                                      Freshney Andy           Ch. Melbourne Mathias
                    Melphis Coruisk                           Freshney Crystal
                                      Cruben Ebb              Cruben Stalwart
                                                              Cruben Miss Seymour
```

Mentor ex Ch. Cruben Melphis Chloe) and he certainly lived up to this promise. During his long career he sired 23 American titleholders and many more in other countries. The list is too long to detail but notice of a few of the more important, because of their effect on the breed, will be offered. His two best known sons, both big winners and useful stud dogs, were Chs. Tulyar of Trenean and Cruben Moray of Clairedale. Unfortunately, the potential of neither dog was fully explored. In spite of this, Moray sired some four U.S. titlists and several others in Canada and England. If the pedigrees of many current winners were extended, Moray would be found in the background.

Ch. Tulyar of Trenean was also neglected by the majority of breeders when they could have used his blood to good advantage. As it was, seven U.S. Champions own him as their sire, while many of the top dogs of the nation have his blood in their veins. Some examples: Chs. Elfinbrook Simon, Rhianfa the Rock, Symmetra Snip and Ugadale Artist's Model.

A few more of Dextor's widely known progeny include Chs. Rachelwood Rifle, Rowemore Brora of Kennishead, Triskett's Most Happy Fella, Wishing Well's Brigadoon and Malcolm's Joshua of Mac-A-Dac. Surely, Dextor left an indelible stamp on the breed through his efforts in the ring and at stud. He died at the age of twelve and a half.

Study of Dextor's extended pedigree shows that he carried on the basic Conas blood through Patrician and the Wolvey Poacher branch of the family. Hookwood Mentor, Dextor's sire, was strong in Patrician blood. In fact, almost every present-day Highlander can be traced back to White Don through Patrician and thence back to Conas.

Because of the tremendous upswing in numbers, and our limitation of space, we will not be as detailed in our documenting of the many outstanding stud dogs and brood bitches from about 1960 onwards. However, a few more must be noted and the first is, of course, the incomparable Ch. Elfinbrook Simon (see extended pedigree herein). He is important for many reasons, but mainly because he has broken all existing stud records for the breed. Through the year 1970, according to reliable figures, the dog has already sired 50 titleholders in the U.S. with many more to come. Among these are several illustrious names including the show winner, Ch. Forest Glen Simon Sez Be Brisk, together with Chs. MacTuff O'The Ridge, Merryhart Petti Pants, Royal Tartan Glen O'Red Lodge, Wishing Well's Kar-Ric's Nonsense, Lawrenton Wee Maggie, Wishing Well's Four Leaf Clover, Wishing Well's White Frost and many others. With this start, and with many others well on the way to the title, it is obvious that Simon's lifetime record will be little short of sensational and will not only stamp him as the greatest sire in the breed's history, but may well elevate him into an imposing position with respect to all breeds. Truly, he has made his mark.

Many others deserve notice and these include a number that are getting first mention. In this group we find Ch. Klintilloch Mercury (a Ch. Rachelwood Rivet son ex Ch. Klintilloch Medallion), who has sired a host of good ones including some nine champions. Some of the best known are: Chs. Flogan Fire N'-Soot, D. and D's Dead Ringer and Flogan Fantom. A second dog from the same kennel, Ch. Klintilloch Monopoly (Ch. Rannoch Dune Defiance ex Ch. Klintilloch Monogram) is doing even better with 11 of his get now owning the title. Among them are such dogs as Chs. MacBurr O'The Ridge, Flogan For-Get-Me-Not and Fiddle D Dee. Also active is Ch. Rainsborowe Redvers who had sired seven titlists, four in 1968, including Ch. Kar-Ric's Rainborowe Replica. Ch. Ugadale Artist's Model has done well with six champions to date, and of course there is Ch. Rannoch Dune Down Beat, who already has sired six titlists with more on the way. Unfortunately, as the numbers of top dogs increase, the use of specific dogs as studs generally decreases, that is, there are fewer litters per dog. This means that most dogs will never have the opportunity to become known as a dominant stud force in the breed. Also, there is a tendency, when one is successful in the ring, to use

124

Ch. Elfinbrook Simon.

```
                                                    Eng. Ch. Hookwood Sensation
                                    Eng. Ch. Roslan Rogue
                                                    Rosalan Regina
                    Eng. Ch. Laird of Lochalon
                                                    Eng. Ch. Barrister of Branston
                                    Susan of Northcliff
                                                    Lucinda of Laurinar
    Eng. Ch. Calluna the Laird
                                                    Calluna Bingo
                                    Calluna Gorbals Diehard
                                                    Calluna Vermintrude
                    Calluna Sheenagh
                                                    Eng. Ch. Shiningcliff Simon
                                    Calluna Sae Sonsie
                                                    Calluna Susan
Ch. Elfinbrook Simon
                                                    Ch. Cruben Dextor
                                    Ch. Tulyar of Trenean
                                                    Heathcolne Thistle
                    Tulyar's Boy
                                                    Ch. Cruben Dextor
                                    Penelope Chorta
                                                    Bright Eyes
    Ichmell Gay Miss
                                                    Eng. Ch. Calluna the Poacher
                                    Eng. Ch. Famecheck Happy Knight
                                                    Famecheck Fluster
                    Famecheck Lucky Star
                                                    Freshney Ratmar
                                    Famecheck Paddy Scalare
                                                    Freshney Futurist
```

one's own dog as a kennel stud rather than shipping a bitch to some distant point for service. This is generally short-sighted for there is no substitute for the proper blending of bloodlines and the inconveniences brought about by shipping will often be repaid many times by the resulting litter. In any event, these conditions appear to level out the records of present day studs and leave one with so many deserving dogs that specific mention of only a few would be unfair. For this reason the listing is of historical interest only as contemporary studs have not been catalogued.

Before leaving the general subject of bloodlines and producers, a word should be said about producing bitches. The female lines are not as easily traced as the male; nevertheless, through the years, the bitches have done their part to further breed interests. In fact, it is generally conceded that the bitch is probably the most important part of any program. Because of the limitations imposed by nature, however, a bitch can only cooperate in the production of a few offspring, while a good stud dog's opportunities in the same direction are almost unlimited.

The aforementioned Culaig must necessarily take first place among producing bitches, with Ch. Morven and Dunollie Admiral to her credit. These two would be a credit to any Highlander. Coming to more recent times, the bitch Ch. Ornsay Vera of Edgerstoune, when bred to Ch. Ray of Rushmoor, whelped a litter that eventually resulted in three champion progeny. These were Chs. Edgerstoune Rowdy, Ringlet, and Requa. The next producer was another Edgerstoune bitch, Ch. Wolvey Pace of Edgerstoune, who, when bred to Ch. Edgerstoune Roughy, became the dam of Chs. Robinridge Commodore, Countess, and Cherie. Still another was Rosalie of Rushmoor, who was twice bred to Wolvey Poacher with tremendous results. Her first litter included Ch. Wolvey Prophet of Edgerstoune, Ch. Wolvey Privet of Edgerstoune, and Ch. Heather

126

Hill Patrick; while her second litter brought forth Ch. Edgerstoune Rohays and Ch. Edgerstoune Raoul.

Several other bitches have produced well; for example, Chs. Clint Casserole and Edgerstoune Raith had the honor of whelping three champions each, although not by the same dog. Edgerstoune Stardust produced Chs. Highland Ursa Major, Highland Sagittarius, Highland Mercury, and Highland Venus in two different litters by Belmertle Aldrich. Ch. Heather-Tyke's Wee Winnie returned four champions in two litters by the same dog when she whelped Chs. Heather-Tyke's Orlando, Ochone, Olivia, and Duncan. And Ch. Belmertle Imogene was the dam of Chs. Humby's Canis Major, Canis Minor, Inverary Charlemagne, and Maxwelton's Promise True.

Ch. Cranbourne Amanda produced four champion offspring (Chs. Cranbourne Arial, Agatha, Alice and Annabelle) by three different dogs; Highland Aries whelped three; and three Klintilloch bitches, Chs. Klintilloch Radiance, Molly Dee, and Mar-Gee, all were the dams of three or more.

More recently a number of bitches have produced extremely well. Among these, one finds Miss Hayward's Ch. Huntinghouse Starmist with four champion get including Chs. Huntinghouse Starflight, Huntinghouse Piperette, Huntinghouse Lucie (all by Elfinbrook Simon) and Ch. Huntinghouse Heather (fathered by Ch. Wishing Well's Brigadoon). Mrs. Eisenberg had a prolific maternal line established through her Ch. Wigtown Margene who whelped Chs. Ability, Creampuff, E-Z Pickens, Chatterbox and Foolish Fancy all with the Kar-Ric's prefix. Foolish Fancy in turn produced Chs. Kar-Ric's Gimlet, Kar-Ric's Nobility, Wishing Well's Kar-Ric's Nonsense and Kar-Ric's Gamble. Gamble then became the dam of Chs. Kar-Ric's O'Please, Thank You, Rainsborowe Replica and Top of The Morning, truly an interesting line of producing dams.

Mr. and Mrs. Ron Davis owned a great producer in Ch. Kirkaldy's Roxanne who when mated to Elfinbrook Simon mothered four champion offspring: Chs. Jenessey's Sir Guy, Myney, Wynken and Spartan Spirit. Another top dam was Ch.

127

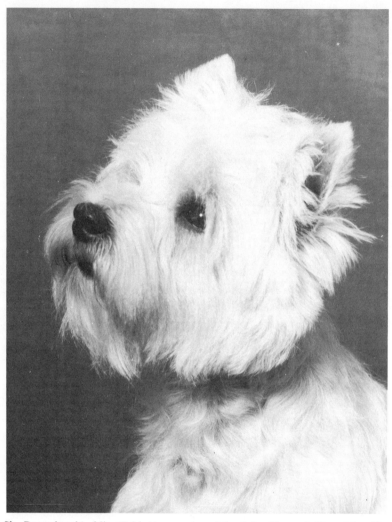

Ch. Donnybrook's Miss Triskett, owned and bred by Mr. and Mrs. John T. Ward, is one example of a useful brood bitch that is an asset to a breeding program. "Trissy" is the dam of eight champions in only two litters.

Lawrenton Wee Maggie, a Simon daughter, who produced five champion offspring by two different dogs. Mated to Ch. Snowcliff Patrician she had Chs. Wishing Well's Holiday Fling, Wee Winklot and Water Baby, while in union with Ch. Triskett's Most Happy Fella she produced Chs. Battison Belladona and Battison Good Friday. Her daughter, Ch. Wishing Well's Water Baby turned out to be another of the leading producers with Chs. MacTuff O'The Ridge, MacRowdy O'The Ridge and Wishing Well's Betsy O'The Ridge (all by Simon, her grandfather), and Chs. MacBurr O'The Ridge and Rona O'The Ridge (the last two by Ch. Klintilloch Monopoly and Ch. MacFife O'The Ridge respectively).

An outstanding breed record was set by Ch. Shiningcliff Donark Dancer, who whelped a total of seven that ultimately made the title. All were Maxwelton dogs and carried the prefix. They were Chs. Maxwelton Coquette, Majorette, Minuet, Shiningcliff Sage, Shiningcliff Sixpence, Simply Sim and Simply Simon. This output sets the "Dancer" apart since she also had time during her spectacular career to win two best in shows.

The listing of producing bitches falls in the same category mentioned with dogs. It is of an historical nature and no attempt has been made to bring the record up-to-date. The numbers now involved are far too great and many deserving animals would have to be left out. Suffice it to say, the distaff side of the breed continues to have its stars and is equally as outstanding as the male side when it comes to producing.

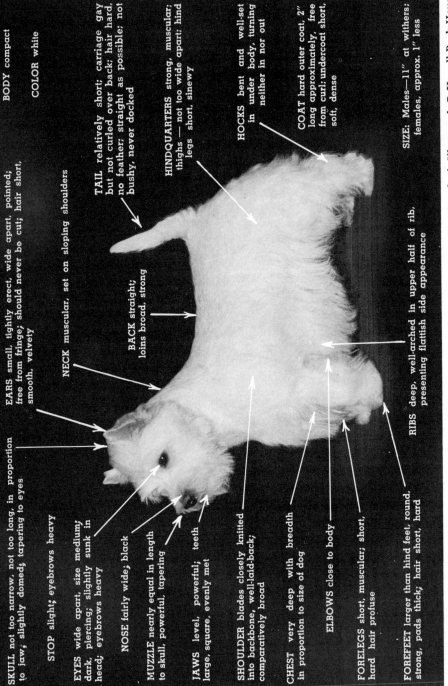

SKULL not too narrow, not too long, in proportion to jaw; slightly domed; tapering to eyes

STOP slight; eyebrows heavy

EYES wide apart, size medium; dark, piercing; slightly sunk in head; eyebrows heavy

NOSE fairly wide; black

MUZZLE nearly equal in length to skull, powerful, tapering

JAWS level, powerful; teeth large, square, evenly met

SHOULDER blades closely knitted into backbone, well-laid-back; comparatively broad

CHEST very deep with breadth in proportion to size of dog

ELBOWS close to body

FORELEGS short, muscular; short, hard hair profuse

FOREFEET larger than hind feet, round, strong, pads thick; hair short, hard

EARS small, tightly erect, wide apart, pointed; free from fringe; should never be cut; hair short, smooth, velvety

NECK muscular, set on sloping shoulders

BACK straight; loins broad, strong

BODY compact

COLOR white

TAIL relatively short; carriage gay but not curled over back; hair hard, no feather; straight as possible; not bushy, never docked

HINDQUARTERS strong, muscular; thighs — not too wide apart; hind legs short, sinewy

HOCKS bent and well-set in under body, turning neither in nor out

COAT hard outer coat, 2" long approximately, free from curl; undercoat short, soft, dense

RIBS deep, well-arched in upper half of rib, presenting flattish side appearance

SIZE: Males—11" at withers; females, approx. 1" less

Visualization of the West Highland White Terrier Standard, reprinted with permission from *Dog Standards Illustrated*, © Howell Book House, 1975.

Official Breed Standard of the West Highland White Terrier

(Submitted by the West Highland White Terrier Club of America,
and approved by the Board of Directors of the American Kennel
Club, December 10, 1968.)

General Appearance:
The West Highland White Terrier is a small, game, well-balanced, hardy-looking Terrier, exhibiting good showmanship, possessed with no small amount of self-esteem, strongly built, deep in chest and back ribs, straight back and powerful hindquarters on muscular legs, and exhibiting in marked degree a great combination of strength and activity. The coat should be about 2 inches long, white in color, hard, with plenty of soft undercoat. The dog should be neatly presented. Considerable hair should be left around the head to act as a frame for the face to yield a typical Westie expression.

Color and Pigmentation:
Coat should be white, as defined by the breed's name. Nose should be black. Black pigmentation is most desirable on lips, eye-rims, pads of feet, nails and skin.
Faults: Any coat color other than white, and nose color other than black, are serious faults.

131

Coat:

Very important and seldom seen to perfection; must be double-coated. The outer coat consists of straight hard hair, about 2 inches long, with shorter coat on neck and shoulders, properly blended.
Faults: Any silkiness or tendency to curl is a serious fault, as is an open or single coat.

Size:

Dogs should measure about 11 inches at the withers, bitches about one inch less.
Faults: Any specimens much over or under height limits are objectionable.

Skull:

Should be fairly broad, being in proportion to his powerful jaw, not too long, slightly domed, and gradually tapering to the eyes. There should be a defined stop, eyebrows heavy.
Faults: A too long or too narrow skull.

Muzzle:

Should be slightly shorter than the skull, powerful and gradually tapering to the nose, which should be large. The jaws should be level and powerful, the teeth well set and large for the size of the dog. There shall be 6 incisor teeth between the canines of both lower and upper jaws. A tight scissors bite with upper incisors slightly overlapping the lower incisors or level mouth are equally acceptable.
Faults: Muzzle longer than skull. Teeth much undershot or overshot are a serious fault, as are teeth defective or missing.

Ears:

Small, carried tightly erect, set wide apart and terminating in a sharp point. They must never be cropped. The hair on the ears should be short, smooth and velvety, and trimmed free of fringe at the tips.

132

Faults: Round-pointed, drop, broad and large ears are very objectionable, as are mule-ears, ears set too closely together or not held tightly erect.

Eyes:
Widely set apart, medium in size, dark in color, slightly sunk in the head, sharp and intelligent. Looking from under heavy eyebrows, they give a piercing look.
Faults: Too small, too full or light-colored eyes are very objectionable.

Neck:
Muscular and nicely set on sloping shoulders.
Faults: Short neck or too long neck.

Chest:
Very deep and extending at least to the elbows, with breadth in proportion to size of the dog.
Fault: Shallow chest.

Body:
Compact and of good substance, level back, ribs deep and well arched in the upper half of rib, presenting a flattish side appearance, loins broad and strong, hindquarters strong, muscular, and wide across the top.
Faults: Long or weak back; barrel ribs; high rump.

Legs and Feet:
Both forelegs and hind legs should be muscular and relatively short, but with sufficient length to set the dog up so as not to be too close to the ground. The shoulder blades should be well laid back and well knit at the backbone. The chest should be relatively broad, and the front legs spaced apart accordingly. The front legs should be set in under the shoulder blades with definite body overhang

133

before them. The front legs should be reasonably straight and thickly covered with short hard hair. The hind legs should be short and sinewy; the thighs very muscular and not set wide apart, with hocks well bent. The forefeet are larger than the hind ones, are round, proportionate in size, strong, thickly padded, and covered with short hard hair; they may be properly turned out a slight amount. The hind feet are smaller and thickly padded.

Faults: Steep shoulders, loaded shoulders, or out at the elbows. Too light bone. Cowhocks, weak hocks, and lack of angulation. A "fiddle-front" is a serious fault.

Tail:

Relatively short, when standing erect it should never extend above the top of the skull. It should be covered with hard hairs, no feather, as straight as possible, carried gaily but not curled over the back. The tail should be set on high enough so that the spine does not slope down to it. The tail must never be docked.

Faults: Tail set too low; tail too long or carried at half mast or over back.

Movement:

Should be free, straight and easy all around. In front, the leg should be freely extended forward by the shoulder. The hind movement should be free, strong and fairly close. The hocks should be freely flexed and drawn close under the body; so that when moving off the foot the body is thrown or pushed forward with some force.

Faults: Stiff, stilty, or too wide movement behind. Lack of reach in front, and/or drive behind.

Temperament:

Must be alert, gay, courageous and self-reliant, but friendly.

Faults: Excess timidity or excess pugnacity.

134

Evaluation and Interpretation
of the Breed Standard

The Standard of Perfection of any breed of dog is the specification set forth by proponents of the breed and recognized by the governing kennel club. Thus, when the West Highland White Terrier was admitted to The American Kennel Club Stud Book as a recognized breed of dog, a Standard of Perfection was submitted, which, upon approval, became the specification for judging and breeding. This Standard was copied closely from that used by the English Kennel Club and set forth desirable and undesirable points in the breed which could be used as a guide both for judges and breeders.

The Standard is an important factor in the success of any breed. If it is sufficiently specific, it is easy to understand and leaves few points of controversy among breeders and judges. On the other hand, if the Standard is ambiguous or sketchy, it causes much consternation among novices, and untold arguments among more serious fanciers. Therefore, a specific, clear, and full Standard is of great benefit to a breed.

The Standard originally adopted by the West Highland

White Terrier Club of America changed little during the first forty years of its use, except in the matter of weight. The top limit was reduced from twenty pounds to eighteen pounds; otherwise, no changes were made until recently, when extensive revisions were carried out by the parent specialty club. The old Standard was fairly specific but contained various passages difficult to reconcile with present day practices. One of these was directed to trimming. The Standard stated that the head and neck should be thickly covered with hair; yet most winning dogs were trimmed about the neck and in other places, in spite of the fact that trimming was specifically not allowed by the Standard. To effect clarification of this, and other points, the West Highland White Terrier Club of America made changes in 1948, 1950 and 1968, rectifying ambiguities and making the entire Standard clearer, both for breeders and for judges. The original Standard in the United States followed closely the original English specifications. The revised form is slightly different but maintains the same attributes as being desirable for the perfect dog; that is, the general type and conformation of the dog remain unchanged.

Basic Factors

When judging a dog of any breed, type, character, and balance are important points to consider. Any dog that lacks type, breed character, and balance is not a good specimen even though his conformation is good, point by point. This is the reason that judging by the point system fails in many cases. Few Standards give much weight to type and character and overall balance, but stress various purely structural points. A dog may be perfect in each of these, but, if the overall structure is not in balance, it is not a good specimen. Therefore, always look for type, character, and balance first and then for specific structural factors. Holland Buckley said all of this in a few words when he remarked, "We must first strike for the true type of the breed, and bring our purely fancy points in afterwards."

136

The basic factors in any breed are founded upon the use of the dog. The Westie is primarily a working Terrier. He was bred to outlast vermin of all sorts and under all conditions. For these reasons, the factors in the Standard which are required for proper work should be considered of utmost importance when breeding or judging.

In order to do his work, the Highlander must be endowed with certain basic necessities—he must be of proper temperament, i.e., have a fearless nature, not quarrelsome but unafraid of man or beast. He must be of proper size so as to be able to go into the cairns and caves of his prey where entrances are small and exits are often even smaller. He must be armed with strong teeth set in powerful jaws so that he can defend himself in a fight to the death. He must own a good double coat, one profuse with soft undercoat and well thatched with a tough and harsh outer jacket that will shed rain or snow and will protect against briars, teeth, and cold. He must have the strong, moderately short back and adequate hindquarters so necessary to any Terrier to aid in holding his prey to the ground. And, above all, he must have good, strong legs terminating in feet carrying thick, tough pads, because the Westie is an earth dog, a digger, and without this equipment he is useless for his purpose. In addition to these, a Terrier of any breed needs sharp eyes, moderately small and dark in the case of the Highlander, and well protected against injury, beneath a strong overhanging brow.

These points may be termed basic factors, since they are of real importance if the dog is to do its work. It is believed that these points should be considered of greater relative importance than others which merely contribute to the beauty of the dog. Therefore they should be carefully evaluated by anyone judging the breed.

Interpretation of the Standard leaves the breeder wide latitude. It has always been thus and is the same in all breeds. The type of a breed becomes modified through judging trends which only reflect the personal interpretation of a Standard by breeders and judges. For these reasons, the Standard will be interpreted here in light of present-day trends as a help to the tyro and to illustrate the degree of latitude which may be taken with certain measurable points.

Size:

The West Highland White Terrier is a medium sized dog. The majority of today's winners range from fourteen to eighteen pounds, with bitches being near the lower limit and dogs near the upper. The Standard does not specify weight but, rather, states that a Westie dog should measure about eleven inches at the withers (shoulder), with bitches about one inch less. A dog that is properly balanced and that measures eleven inches at the withers will generally weigh about 17–18 pounds. The old Standard, before revision, specified the height at the withers between 8 and 12 inches, which gave too much latitude. This does not mean that a dog of 10 or 12 inches at the withers cannot win. He can if his quality is high, but the suggested height of eleven inches is preferred.

Head:

In the matter of heads, a long foreface is to be shunned. Some dogs are seen on the bench with this fault, but it is certainly not to be perpetuated. Balance between foreface and skull, with about equal length for each, is the desirable condition, and overly long heads are also to be discouraged. A Westie is not a white Scottish Terrier—the foreface is rather pointed and is not so wide as to give a "bully" expression. Rather, the effect should be somewhat "foxy." Colonel Malcolm goes into some detail on this point in his monograph on the breed.* He contends that a dog with a reasonably light fore-jaw has a definite advantage in a fight and certainly the winning dogs follow this general plan. The skull is rather short and thick in

* *The West Highland White Terrier,* by Col. E. D. Malcolm, about 1909

138

Correct, wide set, well-carried.

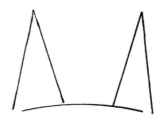

Overly large, but properly set on and carried.

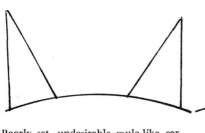

Poorly set, undesirable mule-like carriage.

Too highly set, too close together.

comparison to the exaggerated Scottish Terrier skull. The skull should be slightly domed between the ears and have a definite stop. The ears should be sharp pointed, tightly erect, and should be as small as possible, set wide apart rather than well up on the head like those of a Scottish Terrier. They should not be "mule" ears but should be set upright. Ears poorly placed or carried ruin the expression of a Westie and often make the head look overly long.

The nose must be jet black, although the color will often fade out to a pinkish black during the winter months. This is termed "winter nose" and is noticed in many other breeds of dog. The condition is probably caused by a lack of sunshine.

The teeth of the Westie should be large for the size of the dog and are preferably even in bite with a tight scissors bite being altogether acceptable. Slightly undershot or overshot teeth should be moderately penalized, but, unless the jaws are of improper length, should not carry any heavy penalty. In this connection, it will be noticed that the incisor teeth of many dogs grow out of the jaw at an angle and thus cause an overshot or undershot condition even though the canine teeth mesh perfectly and there is no abnormality in the jaw structure. Dentists have been enlisted to straighten many mouths of this character. Such action is not recommended, since, if the teeth can be straightened, they are not sufficiently out of line to draw any heavy penalization in the ring. There should be six incisors in both the upper and lower jaws.

Pigmentation:

The roof of the mouth and the lips of the average Westie are black, mottled black, or pinkish black. The same is true of the pads of the feet, although a pink pad is occasionally noticed. Black toe nails and black pigmentation on the stomach are also desirable, although many good dogs lack full black nails. I was told by a reputable breeder that the pigmentation sometimes fades out. In the specific case, it was in the toe nails, which

140

were black until four years of age and then gradually turned pinkish in color. This fact is mentioned for what it is worth and may ease someone's mind in the future if a similar condition arises. Black points on the ears are also noticeable in many dogs. This occurs as a blackish coloration on the inside of the ear tips.

The pigmentation of a Westie develops at an early age. For example, newly born puppies generally show pigmentation and usually turn black at their pads within a few days after birth. Black masks around the nose are also noticeable early, and even the nose usually turns black within a few days. This condition is not common among most breeds of dogs, where the pigmentation in the nose usually requires from four to eight weeks for full development.

Depth and extent of pigmentation probably have a marked effect on the sight and hearing of the dog. Many white dogs, such as the Bull Terrier, tend to go blind and deaf through lack of pigmentation; in fact, this defect is found to be a congenital weakness. In this case, however, it should be pointed out that the Bull Terrier is a dominant-black dog bred to the color of white, which accounts for the undesirable heavy ticking black body spots that often occur. The Westie, on the other hand, is a dominant-white dog, and this factor may have considerable bearing on its sight and hearing. In fact, it is said that the Westie and the Samoyed are the only dominant-white dogs existent.* Neither of these breeds has ever exhibited tendencies toward blindness or deafness. In any event, breeders should maintain the heavy pigmentation in the Westie at all times and definitely breed towards, rather than away from, black points.

The eyes of the Highlander are his expression. If they are not of the right size or color, or are poorly placed, the expression is lost. In general, the eyes should be set widely apart, of moderate size, and of a deep hazel color. They should not be a beady black nor should they resemble large soft yellow saucers. One of the most prevalent faults today is overly large eyes with a soft

* *The Bull Terrier,* by Dr. E. S. Montgomery

expression. A Westie's eyes should be of the correct size and color and should have the piercing, pert, and inquisitive expression characteristic of the breed. The rims around the eyes should be black.

Tail:

The tail is a subject of some controversy. The Standard calls for a tail that is relatively short and that does not extend above the top of the skull. However, this point is of small import if the dog is in balance. The length of the tail has, in a great measure, a bearing on the overall outline of the dog, and, in this respect, longer tails will be in better balance on large dogs than on small. The tail should never be docked to attain shortness.

Body Construction:

The legs and feet of the Highlander are of great importance. These extremities are not only his motive power but also his digging equipment. The front feet should be somewhat larger than the back, and all feet should be generously padded with thick strong pads. The front legs are reasonably straight, with elbows close in to the body whether standing or moving. The feet generally toe out slightly, and most dogs, being shown, exhibit this condition, and the Standard permits this deviation. Most short-legged Terriers tend to toe out, and the condition should not be penalized, for it is natural and is brought about by the work for which the dog was bred. F. M. Ross, writing on the Cairn Terrier, states· "No Cairn however deep or in what kind of soil he goes to ground, ever closes himself in. This may be attributed to the turned out feet which help move the earth sideways instead of directly behind the digging dog. Cairns, Westies, Scotties that work should all have this type of foot although accentuated turning out detracts from appearance and does not aid materially to the working character of the dog."

Tail Sets

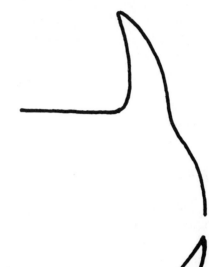

Proper tail set and carriage.

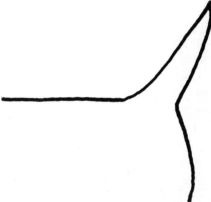

Proper set-on but poorly carried.

Poorly set and carried tail.
Set-on too low.

This passage is a sound evaluation of the reason for the condition and also limits the toeing out to a degree that does not detract from overall appearance.

The hind feet are generally carried rather close together during movement or on standing. Some dogs show a tendency towards wider-spread hind legs, but this is not suggested by the Standard, although it is generally desirable in Terrier breeds. The quarters themselves should be powerful and rugged and capable of propelling the dog over rough terrain with the greatest of ease.

Movement:

Shoulders are vitally important in all breeds. Close knit, well laid back shoulders make for good movement, give good length of neck, and produce apparent shortness of back. Well laid back shoulders are a necessity if the dog is to be a "topper." Upright shoulders spoil the neck line and generally lengthen the appearance of the body and back.

Little has been said or written about true Westie gait; in fact, it seems that few really know the proper gait for the breed. Too often one sees stilted, tight movement with short, rapid steps devoid of drive rather than the free, powerful movement that is so necessary.

A Highlander that has the good lay-back of shoulder and proper rear angulation has a gait that is absolutely distinctive, a gait that approaches a jaunty bounce.

Westies do not generally have the accentuated angulation of long-legged Terriers and this condition contributes to the bounce. But they must have sufficient angulation to have drive so that they cover ground, instead of "standing in their tracks" even though their legs are moving.

Proper front bone construction also contributes to typey breed movement. Well laid back shoulders permit a good forward reach, giving the dog a longer stride which coordinates with proper rear movement.

144

Shoulder Angulation

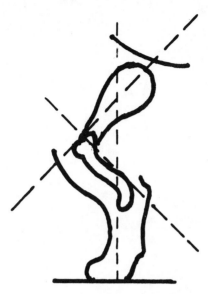

Correct layback of shoulder and its effect on reach of neck, length of back and overhang of body.

Upright shoulder placement makes the neck appear upright and short, back long and destroys the smooth outline between neck and body.

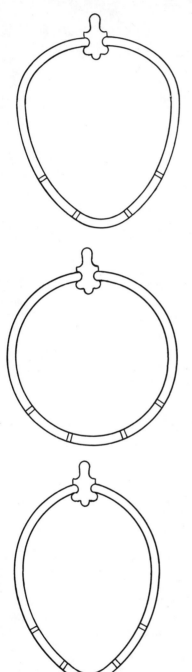

Proper, heart-shaped rib, well-sprung
from backbone, adequate heart room
and good depth.

Round rib without depth. Improper.

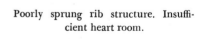

Poorly sprung rib structure. Insuffi-
cient heart room.

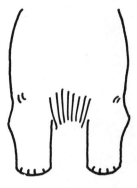

Pinched, narrow front.   Crooked legs. Out at elbow.   Out at elbow.
Fox Terrier-like

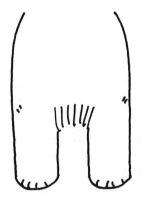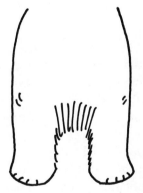

Straight front of proper width.   A proper front. Generally straight
Generally acceptable.   legs, proper width and feet turning
out slightly.

147

Hindquarters

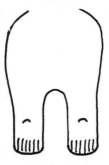

Correct quarters, legs properly spaced,
hocks turned neither in nor out.

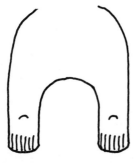

Hindlegs spaced too far apart, otherwise good.

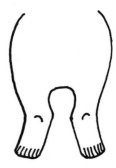

Poor hindquarters, hocks turned in
(cowhocks).

The body of a Westie differs from that of many other Terriers in that it appears more or less flat-sided. The dog is not supposed to have a great, rounded spring of ribs to yield the "big barrel" so desired in some dogs. The Westie's ribs are well sprung from the backbone but taper in quickly in a heart-like shape to give a flattish side appearance. Adequate heart and lung capacity is obtained by depth of rib. Many persons, those who are not informed, penalize a correctly ribbed Westie, but, according to the Standard, a flattish side appearance is correct.

Coat:

The coat is of great importance and too great emphasis can-

148

not be laid on this point. The coat should consist of a soft profuse undercoat and a rather long, hard, and dense outer coat. This outer coat, according to the Standard, should be about two inches long and straight without any tendency towards curl. Hard coats seldom curl; they sometimes have a slight wave which is not too objectionable, but they should never be curly. The color of the coat should be white. No deviation from this color is allowed by the Standard, although many dogs, winning ones at that, have an off-white coat or yellowish dorsal streaks which are apparent even after chalking. In some dogs, this condition is transitory depending on length of coat. In others, the streak of off-color hair is carried by the strain and such color may even be noticed around the ears. This coloring, while not desirable, is not considered too objectionable, particularly since dogs with this slight blemish usually have hard coats. Most soft coated dogs have white coats and when the two faults are evaluated, the off-color is the lesser of the two evils. Many of the good dogs of the day have coats of unimpeachable white, thus proving that proper color in coats can be bred.

In the matter of overall appearance, the West Highlanders should stand off the ground rather than being squat and very short-legged. This does not imply that the Highlander should be long-legged, but he should clear the ground rather than approach the low slung appearance of the Scottish Terrier. Many Westies are too short-legged to look in balance; some few may be termed "leggy." In any case, the most desirable condition is a "happy medium," with legs not too short and not too long. When this condition prevails, the dog appears shorter and more compact without "cloddiness."

This discussion has been set forth to give the novice a few pointers regarding the interpretation and evaluation of the Standard. Desirable points have been stressed and certain factors that are prevalent today have been mentioned. It is hoped that this discourse may be of some aid in evaluating your stock.

149

Barr's Katie McLeod, C.D., C.D.X., U.D., with her owner, Mrs. Margaret Barr, and Obedience Judge Blanche Saunders, receiving award for highest scoring dog or bitch in Utility Class, 1957.

The West Highland White Terrier and Obedience Work

Recent trends among dog show enthusiasts have pointed to increased activity in obedience work. Since the beginning of obedience classes at American Kennel Club shows (1936), this phase of the exhibition has taken on additional yearly importance. In 1936, few shows offered obedience classes, but the reception of these classes made other clubs realize the tremendous spectator appeal of the work. With this in mind, more and more show giving clubs included obedience classes on their show agenda until today few fixtures fail to have such classes. The number of dogs competing has also taken a phenomenal rise. Degree holders in obedience work have become quite numerous and the remarkable part of the entire program resides in the fact that any breed of dog can compete successfully and in most cases does compete. In fact, according to the latest figures released by the American Kennel Club, 10,858 dogs were awarded obedience degrees during 1975 compared to 9,704 bench show champions being awarded their titles during the same period. This shows that obedience work is fast overtaking bench activity, and it indicates that interest in this type of exhibition is real and lasting.

No one breed holds a corner on intelligence. Chihuahuas, Great Danes, Cocker Spaniels, Terriers, etc., all compete side by side with equal success. At one time it was believed that the

151

working breeds, particularly the German Shepherd, Doberman Pinscher, and Boxer, were the most easily trained. This belief was soon changed, since many of the early obedience trial enthusiasts used Standard Poodles in their work. It was not long before all breeds were in competition.

West Highland White Terriers are particularly adapted to the work, since the one requisite that makes training easy is to have an intelligent and yet reasonably calm and tractable dog. Excitable dogs can be trained, but their period of schooling must be longer and the teaching is a bit more harsh on the trainers' nerves and patience. Westies, since they are an inherently calm breed, are quite biddable and therefore train easily with a minimum of lost patience.

Training a dog for obedience has many desirable points. First and foremost, it gives you a dog of which you can be justly proud—an obedient animal that is a pleasure to walk or take visiting. Second, it is a safeguard for the dog itself. A trained dog obeys its master; if told to "sit," it will do so, or if told to "come," its instant reaction is a pleasure. Thus, when an emergency does occur, on the street or in the home, the dog can be made to do the right thing for its own safety by spoken command.

Obedience training is worthwhile for show stock or house pets. It makes all of them better dogs and a greater pleasure to own. In general, novice obedience training is concerned with "heeling" on and off the lead; "sitting" on command or upon the trainer's stopping; coming on recall to a sitting position before the trainer and then heeling to a sitting position at the trainer's left side upon command; a long sit and a long down and a stand stay for inspection, which consists of the dog standing on command in one position until recalled. In an obedience trial a dog must gain a score of 170 out of a possible 200 points on these exercises without scoring less than 50% in any exercise. To gain the Companion Dog degree (C. D.), three such passing scores must be made under at least two different judges. The value of taking a pet through to a degree is obvious. It gains poise for the dog and its trainer and makes the dog work in company with other dogs and in the tumultuous atmosphere of a dog show. When a dog passes the tests under show conditions, he is usually well trained.

Advanced degrees may also be obtained after completion of C. D. work. Companion Dog Excellent (C. D. X.) is the next step, and this work is directed to the above-mentioned exercises together with retrieving over a hurdle, hurdling and broad jumping, and doing the long sit and long down with the owner out of sight and for a longer period of time. Utility Dog (U. D.) is the highest degree and includes all of the C. D. X. tests plus identification of objects by scent and identification of objects of wood, leather, and metal. A tracking degree may also be obtained by causing the dog to follow an outdoor trail by scent alone, and this adds the letter "T" to the U. D. title. Few tracking tests are held and still fewer dogs hold the degree, although interest increases each year.

In spite of the adaptability of the Westie towards obedience work, relatively few have been taken into the obedience ring. This cannot be explained, although the breed did not take long to make the news after the inception of obedience work in 1936. For in 1942, Ch. Robinridge Bimelick made his bench championship and also qualified for a Companion Dog degree. The following year he qualified for his Companion Dog Excellent degree. After this fine start, the pace slowed and other Westies that gained the C. D. degree were few. For example, in 1944, three qualified: Ch. Mi Mon, C. D.; Ch. Mi Evening Lad, C. D.; and Victory, C. D. Mi Bambi, C. D., did it in 1946, followed by Ken Kiltie, C. D., in 1948. After this the C. D. qualifiers were one or two a year and it was not until 1952 that another of the breed made an advanced title. This honor went to Barr's Katie McLeod, C. D., C. D. X. Terrence Dirk, C. D., C. D. X., was the next advanced degree winner, with his C. D. X. title coming in 1955, three years after his C. D. degree.

Finally, in 1956, the ultimate occurred when Barr's Katie McLeod, C. D., C. D. X., added the impressive U. D. to her

153

list of titles. She is the first Westie to earn the Utility Dog degree and was the first of the breed in thirteen years to better the early record of Ch. Robinridge Bimelick, C. D. X. In the years following, relatively few Highlanders have qualified for titles in the work. While the total obedience picture grows rapidly, the degree of Westie participation lags the trend sharply. Through 1975, 255 Highlanders have qualified for the title of Companion Dog (C.D.), 35 for that of Companion Dog Excellent (C.D.X.), 8 for the advanced degree of Utility Dog (U.D.) and only one, Vimy Ridge Catriona, for that of Tracking Dog (T.D.). Thus, the West Highland White Terrier is far behind most other breeds when one considers that a total of 10,858 Obedience degrees were gained among all breeds during the year 1975.

For those who want to train a dog, most large cities have training classes which function throughout the year. These classes are managed by obedience or kennel clubs or by private trainers. When training your first dog for C. D. work it is recommended that you enter such a class, since contact with strange dogs helps in the program. After you have trained one and have the "hang" of training, you can manage alone.

Training a dog is not laborious work. Fifteen minutes a day of concentrated work is all that is required, with about one week's training for each exercise. Thus, in eight to nine weeks' time you can train your dog if you do not shirk your daily duty. When training a dog, do not play with the trainee during work periods. When an exercise is finished, praise the dog and go on to the next bit of work at hand. At the end of the daily training period, praise the dog and let him have a run. Never lose your temper. Sometimes it will seem that the dog will never catch on to a simple exercise, yet, all of a sudden, if you keep working with patience, he will do the exercise perfectly and continue to do so. What is difficult for one dog to learn is easy for another, the whole secret of training being regular work done with authority so that the dog knows it must be done. Never let a dog disobey or not finish an exercise. Keep at it until the job is done correctly.

154

Obedience work should be fun for dog and trainer; for this reason never physically punish a dog. It will spoil his desire to work and no dog that works by fear is a good worker. The happy dog that enjoys the exercises works better and faster than any other, and for this reason great care must be taken during training. After a dog is trained for one degree, it is progressively easier to train him for the next, so keep going.

The mechanics of training will not be discussed here, since there are many tricks that may be used, some on one dog and some on another, to help overcome certain peculiarities. Many good training books are available,* so if you join a training class, it is suggested that you also buy a good book. Your progress will be quicker and your problems will be fewer and will be solved faster.

In obedience work, you will find the exhibitors are fine sports. This may be caused by lack of competition; twenty dogs may be entered in a class and all twenty may receive passing grades. This is unlike showing for conformation where only one dog of a sex can be successful. Even though all dogs in a class may get passing or qualifying scores, there is competitive work among the exhibitors to gain highest scoring in the class. In fact, four place ribbons are given to the four dogs placing first in point of scoring in each class. Whatever the reason, obedience exhibitors are good sports, show interest in your problems, and are ready and willing to help you hurdle any obstacle Your association with this group will be pleasant and the work is enjoyable.

* See Bibliography, page 256.

155

Typical Highlander puppies by Shiningcliff So-So.

Raising, Training, and Conditioning

The care, training, and conditioning of good show stock requires a great amount of time and study. Show dogs do not "just grow" like Topsy. They are brought along carefully, and many a dog that would otherwise become an average specimen may be groomed and nurtured into a show prospect through intelligent care. I do not mean that a poorly conformed specimen can be changed into a winner; I do mean that many an average dog has done well in the ring through care and training, while many a good prospect has been ruined for exhibition purposes through lack of diligence in its rearing.

Puppy Selection

West Highland White Terriers, unlike members of many other breeds, are quite uniform in type, and the Westie breeder is fortunate in having a breed that does not change greatly in quality from the nest to maturity. The average well-bred litter contains several youngsters worth working with for the first five or six months, at which time a more accurate estimate of their potentialities may be made. In choosing the most promising

157

Veteran fancier Mrs. J. H. Daniell-Jenkins with three homebreds. They are (from left) Canadian Ch. Laurie's Piper of the Rouge, Hannijin Hakim of the Rouge and Gale's Bright Gem of the Rouge. Mrs. Daniell-Jenkins, one of Canada's premier breeders, typifies the large number of serious, dedicated individuals who consider breeding good Westies their first priority.

puppies in a litter, it is best to appraise coat, shortness of back, and proportions of head. The cutest puppies, those with the fuzzy coats, generally mature with soft coats requiring untold work to get into show shape and which even then are on the poor side. Of course, if a puppy is otherwise outstanding, the balance may swing in its favor. A relatively short back, strong quarters, well balanced head and good coat are necessities when choosing your future champion, so give plenty of consideration before disposing of surplus puppies. It is a good idea to keep your first litter for at least six months in order to get an idea of how various points develop and retrogress. A little attention given the first litter will afford you valuable information and experience that will pay off in subsequent litters. In this connection, it will aid tremendously in the choosing of promising puppies if you frequently watch the litter at play from a sufficient distance so that your presence is not a distraction. By this observation you can find out which puppy is the leader, the one that is "boss." Such an animal is generally an extrovert and will show well in the ring. You will also be able to observe tail carriage, ear set, and general balance a great deal better than can be accomplished by having the puppies on a table where they are not at ease and are usually very tense. In addition to making these tests, find out which puppies like people the best, which ones come to strangers, and which keep their tails and ears up when being handled. When these individual characteristics of the puppies have been determined, it will often be easier to decide which you want to keep, for a well conformed dog that is shy will be of little use in the ring. Of course, no irrevocable decision on these facts should be made until after six months of age.

Feeding and Exercise

Feeding, first of the dam and then of the puppies, is important throughout the span of a dog's life, and is of utmost importance during the formative stages. For this reason, feed

159

plenty of animal protein food for substance, muscle, and nerves, together with bone building foods and a reasonable balance of carbohydrates, fats, etc. The diet should also contain calcium and vitamin supplements in the form of calcium salts, fish liver oils (preferably fortified), irradiated yeast, etc.

The formation of strong bone and muscle is necessary if the dog is to develop properly. Weak, rickety puppies seldom get the growth required, nor do their legs develop straight and strong. In fact, most weak puppies end up with bench legs, crooked and sorry looking. Old-time breeders appreciated these facts and a poem found in Hugh Dalziel's book *Diseases of the Dog,* written in 1900, is apropos:

"There's some is born with their straight legs by natur,
And some is born with bow legs from the fu'st—
And some that should have growed a good deal straighter,
But they was badly nu'ssed."

The moral is clear: nurse them well (that is, feed properly) and let nature take its course.

Exercise, too, is required by dogs of all ages and can best be given to puppies in a good sized run—either indoor or outdoor, according to the weather. As soon as the youngsters can safely be taken outside, they should be given the benefit of the sun's rays during hours of healthy play. If you can arrange an enclosed run sheltered with plastic-coated wire netting such as is sold for chicken houses, etc., you will be able to give your puppies the benefit of the sun without exposing them to the weather. Such material does not filter out the ultraviolet rays of the sun as does ordinary glass.

Kenneling

The kenneling of Westies when more than two or three are kept is an easy matter. The breed is hardy and healthy and needs no special treatment. Dogs should be kept in separate boxes at night, as shown in the drawing, and should be carried each day to their runs. The runs need not be large, ten or

160

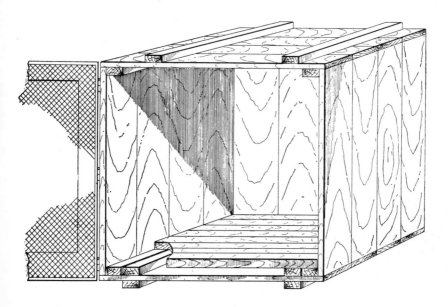

Westie box suitable for house or kennel.

twelve feet long by four feet wide being adequate. Running two dogs together, usually a dog and a bitch, is the best procedure. Each run should have some shade for hot weather and should also have an area that gets sun. Dogs need the run-type exercise for only about two to three hour periods, after which they may be put in their boxes. Exercise in runs should never take the place of road work. Each run should preferably be erected on slightly sloping ground to assure adequate drainage and should be surfaced with gravel, black top or cement. A fence of fox wire or chain link is recommended and should be about four feet high. Every run should also include a platform about fifteen inches high and large enough for the dogs to lie on or under as is their desire.

The kennel building may be any dry and tight enclosure and does not have to be heated except for the comfort of humans. Westies can take heat or cold without discomfort and this ability possibly stems back to their unique background. In their native habitat, living conditions often left much to be desired and a dog that did not have stamina could not have survived. These conditions are best exemplified by remarks made to me by Mr. Walter Reeves when reminiscing about his observations in Scotland at the turn of the century. Mr. Reeves said that he had frequently seen Westies on the rugged beaches of the West Highland of Scotland where they were great favorites of the native fishermen. These tough little Terriers had the rotting remains of an overturned boat for their kennels and their food consisted of what they could hunt, supplemented with fish from their master's catch. Here they lived the year around, wet by the spray of the sea and scorched by the rays of the sun, hunting and scurrying back and forth over the rocks and crags of their beach homes. Small wonder that their descendants, the dogs of today, are so healthy, and obvious is the reason why no Westie requires special care.

In fact, the breed does well in any climate. I have shipped dogs to the tropics, where their owners report that they thrive without discomfort. Others have gone to cold climates with like

162

reports. Of course, we all know that the breed is happy and healthy in the temperate climate of the United States.

With this background it is obvious why the use of heated or air cooled kennels is not recommended for the breed. If, for your own comfort, you feel a necessity for heat in the kennel, try to keep it at about 55 to 60°F and constant.

The kennel should be screened for summer use to keep out flies, and plenty of ventiltaion is advocated. Highlanders can take a great deal of heat if adequate ventilation is provided. In this respect it is suggested that a window fan be used on hot and humid days to keep the inmates comfortable.

An elaborate kennel is very nice to have but it does not improve the quality or comfort of your dogs. A clean kennel, on the other hand, is a necessity if the dogs are to be kept in good condition. Each day, thoroughly clean the boxes and kennel and disinfect with a mild disinfectant. Raising good dogs takes a great deal of hard and intelligent work which is well repaid by the results obtained.

Puppy Care

At about eight weeks of age, strip off all flying, fluffy top coat. This will permit normal growth of healthy hair which will develop into a good, tight, straight coat, a great asset to the dog in later life. Daily grooming of the coat from eight weeks on in the form of brushing will aid immeasurably in improving its texture and bloom.

While working on the coat, it is a good idea to clip the hair off the outside of the ears. This will lighten the ears and make it possible for them to stand erect. As a rule, a puppy's ears will rise normally to a half prick position and then to fully erect. This may occur simultaneously with both ears, or one may go up, followed by the other a few days later. Once up, the ears may drop several times before standing permanently. In general, the ears should go up at from eight to twelve weeks of age.

163

At about six weeks of age puppies should be wormed for ascarids (stomach or round worms). And all puppies should be protected against distemper at an early age.

At approximately four months of age, the average puppy commences to lose its puppy teeth and acquires a permanent set. This teething period continues from one to two months according to the individual puppy. During this time, special attention should be given to the mouth. Experience with Westies has shown that the puppy teeth do not generally fall out as readily as in other breeds. For this reason, if you see a permanent tooth coming in alongside a puppy tooth, quickly extract the offender and give the permanent tooth a chance to grow in straight. Many poor mouths can be attributed to failure to care for the teeth during teething; in reality, the mouth was made poor by the owner's failure to aid nature.

Lack of care can result in some weird conditions. I have seen Westies and Cairns that have had a double set of teeth, the milk teeth with the permanent teeth right beside them. Such a mouth is terrible and could have been avoided by the breeder's taking more care of the puppy. If you cannot remove the teeth yourself, enlist the aid of a veterinarian, although milk teeth generally come out easily, for they have very little root.

Taping the Ears

During the teething period, ears do funny things. Some ears will not stand erect before the puppy teethes, while others that have been up will drop. Personally, I prefer to tape ears that are not erect at four months or which have dropped during teething. This may be done either by rolling them and taping them together at the desired distance or by forming a tape backing for the ears and then taping them together. (See chart.) Either method is satisfactory. Taping strengthens the weak ear cartilage and sets the ears better. It also helps the dog to carry its ears better in later life. Some ears do not stand for a long time, and the taping must be repeated several times. The tape

ALTERNATIVE METHODS FOR TAPING EARS

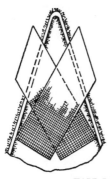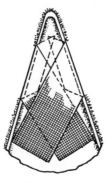

TAPE BACKING ON EAR

Use two or more pieces of tape and apply to each ear as shown. Criss-cross the tape and apply at front of ear as shown. Cup the tape so that ears are upright and then tape ears together as shown.

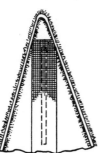

ROLLING EARS

Use a portion of a toothpick as a splint and apply to front of ear as shown with adhesive tape. Next roll ear by wrapping two strips of tape as shown.

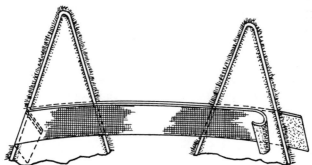

TAPING EARS TOGETHER

After ears have been backed or rolled as shown in the above drawings, set them the proper distance apart with a longer strip of tape as shown here. Apply another strip on other side of ears so that tapes are adhered together. Be sure that ears are free to move, and that tape is not adhered to head hair.

should be left on for a week or ten days and then removed before the ears become sore. Boric acid powder dusted around the base of the ears helps to prevent soreness. I have seen ears that did not stand before ten months of age, but which were stiffly erect when they did stand, so do not give up too soon.

A warning—never tape one ear and not the other. Taping of the ears together causes the ears to work or move simultaneously and thus strengthens both of them; so if one ear is up and the other is down, tape both ears up and then together and the results will be much better.

Where just the tip of the ear falls over, it is sometimes possible to stiffen it by merely coating the ear with collodion, well applied on both inside and out thereof. It will cause no discomfort and may be used on one ear only.

Lead Breaking

At four to five months of age, the puppy is ready for preliminary show training. Lead breaking is the first step. This may be most easily accomplished by first permitting the puppy to wear a light show collar for a day or two. The next step is to attach a lead to the collar and try gently to lead the dog. If he has a mind of his own, and most have, merely hold the lead and let the puppy balk and pull for about ten minutes. Repeat the procedure daily, for a few days, and you will notice that the dog's distrust of the lead lessens and that you can finally lead him around. In about a week's time, the puppy will permit leading for a walk. This should be short at first (as young dogs tire easily), gradually increasing in length until at eight months the puppy is walked about a mile a day in two periods. This early lead training means much in later show experience. You will have a dog who does not fight the lead, moves easily and without fear, and is under complete control. Teach the pup to move on either a loose or a tight lead, at your left side, without pulling. Endeavor also to keep the ears and tail up by constant talking, even bribing with small pieces of liver or

166

Only time will tell what the future can hold for such hopefuls as these. No dog can ever be better than its individual genetic picture, but careful management and thoughtful training will develop in every dog its own maximum potential.

other choice tid-bits. This makes the puppy a good showman and many an inferior dog has beaten a better specimen on show-manship alone. A good dog that does not make the best of itself is a hard animal to judge and is a complete disappointment to its owner, while a good showman is always the "judge's friend."

Let the puppy run about the kennel or house while you are around and always keep a tid-bit in your pocket. Let the dog take a nibble occasionally and, before long, you will have the youngster looking up at you even when being walked. This makes his exhibition a pleasure. During all walks with your puppy, stop periodically and pose him as you would in the ring, make him stand with tail up and ears erect and with his neck well up. This gets him used to ring procedure and adds to his showmanship.

It is also useful to have someone not known to the puppy go over him now and then. This merely requires overall handling of the puppy and does not require special knowledge—anyone can do it. At the same time, have the lips lifted and gums and teeth examined; this will eliminate future antics when the judge wants to look at the teeth.

Lead breaking should be followed by walking your hopeful in congested areas where cars and people pass. This accustoms the puppy to the very atmosphere of a dog show with its excite-ment, noise, and many strangers. A dog that does not shy at such things out-shows one that does.

For several months before starting to show them it is also a good idea to take young dogs for rides in a car and in a crate. In this manner, much of the excitement of their first few shows is removed, as they ride like veterans and are comfortable and used to riding and crating. When first breaking a puppy to this experience, teach him to sleep in a crate by substituting it for his regular sleeping box. After a week of this, and when he is perfectly comfortable in the crate, take him for a short ride in it. Take him to the store or village several times for short rides. After a while he may be taken for longer rides until such time as he is perfectly broken to riding in a crate. By following

168

this course, the puppy arrives at his first show fresh, not sick and scared, which would have been the case had he not been properly broken.

In the event that he tends to be carsick, you may administer a sedative prescribed by your veterinarian before you start out. This will calm his nerves and relieve carsickness to a marked degree. After several rides, you will probably not have to worry, since most dogs are good travelers and like to ride.

Can. and Am. Ch. Roseneath White
Knight

Ch. Cruben Flashback

An appealing headstudy of Ch. Wycote Bramhill Brocade
showing proper head trimming.

Grooming the Westie

Grooming your dog is the most important single item towards good show condition. Grooming should begin at about two months of age and continue throughout the dog's life. Five to ten minutes vigorous brushing every day will do more good for the texture and growth of a dog's coat than any other treatment. It will also stimulate the skin and cause a flow of natural oils, thereby creating a healthy skin condition. At each grooming period, loose flying hairs should be plucked out. But very little combing should be done, since this tends to remove too much undercoat.

In order to further stimulate the growth of hair at selected points, warm olive oil massaged into the skin is good. This is especially helpful around the muzzle as it softens hard furnishings and, thus, prevents whiskers from breaking off. Rain water brushed into the coat is also a growth stimulant and will aid in bringing out the bloom.

Another frequent task concerns nails, which should be cut back with nail clippers and then filed a little each day or two to keep them very short. This is especially true on the front feet since the nails on the rear feet wear off more readily than those in front. Short nails improve a dog's feet and make them more compact, while long nails tend to splay the feet and break down the pasterns. This task should start early, at about eight weeks of age, and continue throughout the dog's life.

Trimming makes a dog look smarter and improves its general appearance just as a hair cut or "hair do" improves the appearance of a man or woman. This operation takes a little time each day, and the best trim may be decided upon by observation and comparison. In all cases, a dog's trim should be personalized; that is, trimming should make the dog look its best by bringing out good points and hiding faults as much as possible.

In answer to the question, "How should a Highlander be trimmed?" the following may be said: A Westie is the same as any other breed that requires trimming of one sort or another. Every dog requires different treatment to make him look his best so as to present him to the judge in the most acceptable condition. One dog requires heavier trimming than another, one requires thinning of the coat where another needs more coat. In other words, trimming must be carried out to suit a specific dog. If a dog is too heavy in front, the hair should be thinned on the shoulders to give the appearance of a proper front. If a dog's tail is low set, hair should be taken off the back of it and grown on the front, and additional coat should be cultivated behind the tail to give the proper appearance. Large-eared dogs need more hair between the ears than small-eared ones. Long forefaced, lean-headed dogs require more frame to the face and heavier whiskers to give the illusion that the head is broader and shorter than it really is. In other words, there can be no set trimming formula, since the actual work on any dog must be done to present that dog in the best light, to accentuate good points and minimize faults.

Actually, trimming is an art—there is no easy way to learn. Experience and knowledge are the only teachers. First, one must know how a good specimen of the breed should look, and

172

second, one must be able to properly fault the dog. With these two situations in hand, the trimming commences. Even now, if you are not adept at using strippers, scissors, and other paraphernalia, you cannot do a finished job. Thus, it is apparent that it requires background and knowledge tempered with more than average experience to do a really good job.

These factors are among the reasons why professional handlers often do better in the ring than those who are not so experienced. The professional's dog is put down properly, while the novice-trimmed animal often is poorly presented. This should not be a discouraging condition but rather a challenge to learn and to do a better job. That there can be no set formula is clearly shown by study of other breeds. Wire Fox Terriers, Scottish Terriers, Kerry Blues, etc., are all trimmed in a custom manner—in a manner to suit the particular dog. That all good dogs of a breed resemble one another is a tribute to the trimmers, since these same dogs if stripped bare would not look alike. Faults would appear that are entirely hidden by expert trimming. A good judge can find these faults, for he not only knows what he is looking for but also he knows the devious ways used to hide faults and with his hands can quickly find the faults. Often one finds a straight-stifled animal, almost Chow-hocked, that appears to have good angulation. Upon inspection, it will be found that much hair has been grown on the back side of the hock and that this hair is trained to stand away from the hock. At the same time, hair has been grown on the thigh to round out an otherwise weak hindquarter. The overall picture is good, but the bone structure is just as bad as before the expert went to work. So it goes: faults are minimized, good points are accentuated, until the dog appears at his best. Two important admonitions, *never* use clippers on the body coat of a dog you wish to show. It will take months and sometimes two complete strippings before the coat regains texture, quality and "lie." Clipping tends to make the coat curl and always leaves it softer in texture. The only time clippers should ever be used is on old pensioners and then only when stripping

173

causes them apparent discomfort. The second admonition concerns the use of thinning shears on the body coat. Increasing numbers of dogs are being seen in the ring where the use of such shears is apparent to all. Steps in the side coat are tell-tale signs of the short-cut and will take months to eliminate. When thinning shears are used at all, they should be used with extreme care and with the lie of the coat, not across it. It is always best to avoid thinning shears and prepare the dog ahead of time so that their use is not required.

The trimming chart suggested for the tidying up of a Westie is about all the help anyone can give. The rest comes with experience, appreciation of conformation, and a knowledge of what is wanted in the breed. In general, since a Westie is not trimmed to extremes, trimming of the ears, frame around face, tail, feathering, and feet will yield a neat appearance. Flying hair on the body should be eliminated if possible, and the dog should be presented as clean and white as possible. The fine points of trimming can only be gained by hard work, mistakes, observation of experts at work, and experience—the same formula that is applied to every other breed that requires trimming.

In this connection, some learn slowly while others have a capacity to learn more quickly. Trimming of feet in itself is an art seldom mastered. Yet, neat feet do more to set off a dog than any other single factor. Much the same is true of tails and ears. These are all important in the trimming of our breed and the art of trimming these parts of the body properly should be mastered first. The rest will come with experience, if you are patient and anxious to learn.

A good dog poorly presented has its chances of winning cut tremendously. This is not because the judge does not know the faults of the dogs in competition but rather because the overall appearance of a dog has a strong bearing on the outcome of the placements. Type is of major importance and dog poorly done up often appears to lack type because of the faulty trim. On the

174

other hand, a reasonably good dog properly put down exemplifies the proper type and even when hidden faults are found, it is difficult to beat him, for the first factor in judging is to pick dogs that look like Westies. For this reason, faulty trimming often spoils the chances of an otherwise good dog.

This commentary on trimming does not answer the question "How should a Westie be trimmed?", because such a question cannot be answered by a general statement. However, any exhibitor who will pick up the challenge and learn through experience, study, and intelligent observation will eventually master the art. One comforting thought is that you can never ruin a dog permanently by trimming; your mistakes will soon be obliterated by new growth of coat. In all cases, the trimming should be moderate so that the dog yields the final appearance of being neat and well trimmed without being overtrimmed. This may be difficult to comprehend but you will get the idea as you work.

Tools used for trimming differ with different handlers but usually include scissors and a stripping or plucking knife or penknife. Scissors may be used for trimming around the ears and feet, although some adept individuals use the knife for all of these operations. Mrs. Pacey, when in this country in 1955, gave a demonstration of trimming a Highlander. She used a sharp penknife and preferred it to any other instrument.

The hair to be removed is grasped between the blade of the knife and the thumb and pulled out. If any is strongly rooted, it will be cut off at varying lengths, eliminating a cut look. Frankly, the knife is excellent, and since Mrs. Pacey's suggestion, I have discarded all other instruments for this inexpensive tool. The knife has another advantage that is lacking in the regular stripping blade—when thinning out coat it is possible to dig in point-wise and take out a few hairs at a time to do a fast and effective job.

A good trimming bench or table is an invaluable aid when working on your dog and also helps to train him for show. The

175

General Trimming Instructions
with Step-by-Step Procedures

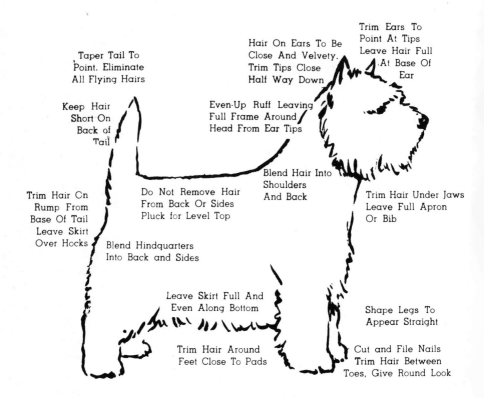

Taper Tail To Point. Eliminate All Flying Hairs

Hair On Ears To Be Close And Velvety. Trim Tips Close Half Way Down

Trim Ears To Point At Tips Leave Hair Full At Base Of Ear

Keep Hair Short On Back of Tail

Even-Up Ruff Leaving Full Frame Around Head From Ear Tips

Trim Hair On Rump From Base Of Tail Leave Skirt Over Hocks

Do Not Remove Hair From Back Or Sides Pluck for Level Top

Blend Hair Into Shoulders And Back

Trim Hair Under Jaws Leave Full Apron Or Bib

Blend Hindquarters Into Back and Sides

Leave Skirt Full And Even Along Bottom

Shape Legs To Appear Straight

Trim Hair Around Feet Close To Pads

Cut and File Nails Trim Hair Between Toes, Give Round Look

Noose from ceiling—or—Trimming Stand

A wire brush mounted in rubber or a stiff bristle brush.

A fairly coarse metal comb of good quality is essential.

A coarse and a fine stripping knife especially for terriers

Thinning shears and barbers scissors for finishing touches.

A good toe nail clipper and a coarse metal file are musts.

YOU don't need much equipment to get the job done. A steady table, tack box or bench at which you can sit or stand comfortably is your first essential. An adjustable leash hanging from the ceiling or a metal bar attached to your tack box or grooming table will be invaluable in keeping your dog in position while you work on him. With your tools handy and a good light on your dog you are ready to begin.

177

table should be of the proper height so that you may stand comfortably while working and should not be too large in area. A table about twenty-five inches long by eighteen inches wide is adequate. Mounted on the side of the table near the front should be an adjustable upright from which can be suspended a slip collar adjustable to the proper height for each dog. This not only aids you in your work but will keep the head up and teach the dog to stand properly.

Instead of an adjustable upright, you may hang a collar from the ceiling directly over the table. This collar may be adjusted for proper height from the table. Either expedient is satisfactory.

Using the wire brush, start at the back of the head and go over the entire body, brushing with the lay of the hair, including the chest, legs and tail, until all tangles, knots and clumps are cleaned out. When your brush meets no resistance you are ready for the metal comb.

Follow the same procedure with the comb until the coat lays flat. Brush and comb the head and face whiskers last as dogs will sometimes resent this. Don't be rough but do be firm and he will get the idea and learn to like it.

Comb hair on top of head forward and upward. Comb the ruff from behind the ears out and forward. Study the effect before doing any trimming in this area.

Trim hair inside of ears close, about half way down from tips. Cut hair on tips of ears close and even, at angle shown to blend into ruff. Trim hair on back of ears about 1″ from tips leaving velvety hair. Leave hair long around base of ears. The idea is to make ears look small and set wide apart.

Comb eyebrows forward and trim on slant as shown. Separate eyebrows slightly with trimming knife and let eyes show. Comb ruff forward and out, then trim both sides even with thinning shears. Leave ruff full but don't overbalance the head with respect to rest of body.

179

Use your thumb and forefinger, or the stripping knife here. Take it easy; the key word is BLEND. Trim lightly on top of neck, starting behind ears and blending into body hair on neck and shoulders. If hair is very thick on sides of neck and shoulders, you may have to use thinning shears here. Taper into shoulders and body.

Clean hair on neck under head down to point of the breast-bone, leaving a bib, or apron of long hair there. Clean on each side of bib to point of shoulders. Note: When using thinning shears always cut with the lay of the hair . . . not across. Take a snip or two, comb out and check before each cut.

180

If hair on neck and back is loose enough to be pulled out easily with the thumb and forefinger, pull it and wait for a new growth to come in. Use your stripping knife to even up the top coat to give the back a straight, level look. If there is a dip in the top line, leave hair full, or if there is a hump, trim close to even up.

Shape the tail to look like an inverted carrot and to appear short as possible. Trim hair on the back of the tail so that it is almost a flat triangle from the tip, blending into the hips. Remove long hair on rump from base of tail to about half-way to the hocks, leaving a skirt between the legs.

Comb hair on legs up then down and study to see where you need to trim to give them that straight, full look when viewed from any direction. Even up feather so that when dog is moving the hair at elbows does not fly out. Trim very lightly. Leg hair grows very slowly.

181

Now cut the hair around the feet close to the pads to give feet a round, full look. This is best done with the dog's weight on the foot. You can make him stand by raising the opposite foot during the trimming. Also trim the hair between the toes.

Using your toe nail clippers cut just the tips of the nails about $\frac{1}{8}''$ being careful not to cut into the quick.

Then use your file to smooth and round off. Dogs don't mind the filing as much as the cutting. Toe nails should be filed as close as possible once a week to keep in shape.

Keep nails short at all times. It improves the feet, and makes the dog more comfortable.

CORRECTING FAULTS:

While you can't actually correct physical faults, you may be able to hide some of them by careful trimming. So, if there is an undesirable curve or dip, leave hair full there to cover.

Comb and brush coat down as flat as possible and then pin a towel on the dog to keep things in place. Use large safety pins to do this, one under the neck, one just back of the front legs and one under the flanks. This will allow for movement but won't permit coat to "fly" or stand up.

Here is the transformation after trimming, showing one side completed and the other side rough:

Trim Ruff From
Ear Tips To
Frame Of Face

Trim Hair Under
Chin To Point Of
Breast Bone

Shape Legs So That They Look
Straight. Even Feather So Hair On
Elbows Won't Fly When Moving

Here is the transformation, looking from the rear after trimming, showing one side completed, and the other side rough:

Shorten Hair
Behind Ears
And Taper Into
Shoulders

Trim Hair On
Rump From
Base Of Tail
Leave Skirt
Over Hocks

When getting your dog ready for show, you had best wash its feet, legs, and whiskers and, if it is hard-coated, you may risk a complete bath occasionally. Otherwise, merely wipe off the dog's coat with a damp Turkish towel rubbed in the direction that the hair lies. The dog should be whitened the day of the show with any of the usual preparations, such as chalk or whiting. A mixture of precipitated chalk, whiting, and boric acid powder in equal parts does a good job, and the boric acid powder keeps the skin from becoming irritated. In accordance with A.K.C. rules, all of this whitening should be thoroughly brushed out of the coat prior to entering the ring.

After the dog has been prepared, it should be towelled down with a Turkish towel pinned beneath the neck and under the tuck-up. This makes the coat lie flat and keeps your entry clean on the bench or in the crate. Just before judging, remove the towel and comb the dog thoroughly to remove every tangle and to separate each hair. A good combing before taking it into the ring makes the dog look well groomed. Remember, you cannot help losing if your dog is inferior anatomically to another exhibit, but never lose because your dog does not show, is not in condition, or is not spotlessly clean. All of these factors are controlled by you and you alone.

Apropos is a remark accredited to the late George Steadman Thomas, well known Anglo-American Terrier expert and judge, who said, "The best looking dog will often beat a better dog put down indifferently."

Westies at the Boardwalk show in 1976. This group offers a typical example of the large numbers of quality specimens that can be found in competition in most areas. The existence of keen competition speaks highly for the breed and the breeders in their efforts to produce and bring to the shows the best they have. *Fred Groves, Courtesy Groves Photography.*

The Value of Dog Shows

What is the value of a dog show? This question is frequently asked when discussing the advisability of entering a dog in one of these events. The answer is simple and the reasons for showing your stock are logical and sound. The only true measuring stick of your breeding progress and success is comparison of the best you have with the best of other breeders. If your dog or dogs win consistently, you can rest assured that the type of dog you breed is desirable and that you are progressing in your breeding program.

Furthermore, showing of dogs keeps you on your toes. The results of the shows are a constant challenge to your ability. If your dogs do not win, or win very seldom, do not be "kennel blind" but begin to look for failings. And when you find them, start to breed away from these faults and so improve your stock. Dog shows are the only opportunity you have for comparison and also the only place that you may obtain unprejudiced criticism, such as a judge's placement of your dog with reference to other dogs. If, after attending three or four shows, you find that all judges have similar reactions towards your entries, rest

187

assured that their opinions, good or bad, are correct, and be guided accordingly.

Dog shows have had a long and varied history and are conducted on different plans in different countries. In England, shows have been in existence for a long time. The first event of the bench type was held for sporting dogs at Newcastle-on-Tyne in 1859. Sixty Pointers and Setters made up the entry. Judges for this historic affair were: Messrs. J. Jobling, T. Robson, E. Foulger, R. Brailsford, and J. H. Walsh ("Stonehenge"). Shows of varying success were held from that time until April 1873, when the English Kennel Club was organized and caused a stabilization of the events which affected their first real bid for prominence. S. E. Shirley, founder of the club, served as its first chairman and later as its first president.

In the United States, early history of shows is obscure, but honor for the first bench show in our country is credited to Hempstead, Long Island, near which place a show was held in 1874. Westminster was the first of the better organized clubs to hold a show, and its initial event was staged May 7th to 11th, 1877, in New York City. The following year, the Boston and Baltimore clubs held shows in addition to the New York fixture. The American Kennel Club was organized September 17, 1884, in Philadelphia, Pennsylvania.

During this general period, dogs in the United States were registered with one or more of several organizations that maintained stud books. The best known was the National American Kennel Club whose stud book was first published in 1878. A partly contemporaneous effort was the American Kennel Register. After organization of the American Kennel Club (1884) and in 1888, the National American Kennel Club records were taken over by mutual consent and became the initial volumes of the present American Kennel Club Stud Book. The Register ceased to exist after February of 1889.

The organization of the American Kennel Club did in the United States what the English Kennel Club accomplished in Great Britain; it stabilized dog show practises by enforcing uni-

188

form rules, and provided an impartial governing body operating for the best interests of purebred dogs and for the benefit of no particular individual or group of individuals.

Dog shows in different countries, under the authority of different kennel clubs, operate in varying manners and award their championships after different requirements have been met. English shows are divided into several classifications, depending on their importance and scope. The only shows that have any bearing on championships are those events termed "championship shows." The remaining fixtures, which are numerically superior, may be likened to our sanctioned matches. The English championship shows are analogous to our licensed or members shows, in that a dog, by winning in its sex and breed, may obtain credit towards its championship. A championship (or challenge) certificate is given to the winner of each sex in each breed at these events. No relationship exists between the number of entries and the certificate awards. This is taken care of by the fact that relatively few championship shows are held each year, thereby assuring a good entry with worthy competition. It requires three such certificate awards under three different judges to qualify for the title of champion.

In the United States, a different system prevails. To become a champion of record, a dog must win 15 championship points under three different judges, including two three-point shows under different judges. The number of points awarded at any given show is dependent on the number of dogs of the sex actually shown in the breed for a given geographical division, of which there are four together with a separate schedule of points for shows held in Alaska and Hawaii. These ratings reflect the number of dogs in each sex of a given breed being shown in the area. These ratings vary in accordance with the division in which the competition occurs and the current schedule of points for all breeds appears in the front of all show catalogs and is published in the *Gazette* annually in the April and May issues. The American Kennel Club annually adjusts the point ratings to keep competition strong and to

189

equalize for changing conditions of popularity. Thus no dog can become a champion too easily; it must score over competition consistent with the number of dogs of its breed currently being shown in the Division. These changes emphasize the constant fluctuations in point ratings that are being made by The American Kennel Club in an effort to keep competition strong and to equalize for changing conditions of popularity.

In general, The American Kennel Club endeavors to keep the number of three, four, and five point shows to about twenty percent of the total shows in a given division. This means that major shows (three point or better) will be available but will not be so numerous that the average exhibitor can finish a dog in three shows. It also means that in a small registration breed, where competition is hard to find, that it will not be impossible to finish a champion, which would be the case were all breeds to have the same rating.

In the early part of the century, the American system was entirely different. At that time, the point rating at any show depended upon the total number of dogs exhibited at the show. Thus, it was actually possible for a dog to win five points without any competition. The ratings for shows were as follows: 1000 dogs and over—five points; 750 to 1000 dogs—four points; 500 to 750 dogs—three points; 250 to 500 dogs—two points; and 250 dogs and under—only one point. The obvious unfairness of this system revolved around the fact that at a one point rating show, a winning dog might beat more dogs of the breed than in some other show where a five point rating prevailed. The present system eliminates these inequities and permits the maximum point rating at any show regardless of size, providing the required number of dogs in the sex of the breed are present.

Canadian championships are acquired in much the same manner as American championships except that only ten points are needed. The other requirements are substantially the same and ratings vary in accordance with the numbers being shown in each breed.

A dog show, its method of procedure and ultimate goal, is

Ch. Vimy Ridge Money Man, owned by Liz Hallmark and bred by her father Clifford Hallmark, shown going best of breed at Westminster 1970 under James A. Farrell, Jr. A son of Ch. Sollershot Sober, Money Man also won the winter specialty the same year. He is handled by his breeder.

Ch. Citrus Picolo Pete, owned by C. W. Burdick and shown by Daisy Austad. An import, he is shown in a win under Elbert E. Vary.

relatively simple to comprehend and is analogous to any other sporting contest where many opponents vie for honors. It is nothing more than an elimination contest where dogs compete in relatively small groups and classes for the purpose of eliminating certain unsuccessful contestants. The winner of each elimination round progresses to the next higher competition for further elimination until only one dog remains, and that dog is awarded the title of best dog in show.

Every dog show is broken down into breed competitions which are usually further subdivided by sexes with five regular classes generally being provided in each sex. The official definitions of the classes may be found in Chapter 6, Sections 3 to 9 inclusive, of *Rules Applying to Registration and Dog Shows* (American Kennel Club).

If you plan to exhibit dogs, endeavor to join a local dog club. Most cities have such an organization and it generally includes a majority of the active exhibitors in the vicinity. Contact with these persons will help you over many rough spots and you can also gain much knowledge through this association.

In general, dog shows are wonderful places to gain knowledge of your breed and dogs in general. Professional handlers and experienced exhibitors may be watched as they prepare their dogs, and their actions in the ring should be noted. Much can be learned in this manner. Most of these persons are willing to assist the novice if asked courteously and at a time when they are not rushed to show or prepare another dog. They were all novices at one time or another, since there is no means yet devised of skipping this phase. Intelligent observation and courteous questioning will aid more than anything else in acquiring the knack of showing dogs.

Much benefit can also be derived by questioning the judge, who may be asked, after the breed judging has been completed, his opinion of your dog. Tell him frankly that you are a novice, and you will receive much help. Remember, however, that judging is a matter of personal interpretation of the Standard and different judges see things differently. Therefore, ask several arbiters the same question and use the overall picture given by them to determine just where your dog excels or fails.

One more word on the subject of dog shows. These events, while awesome the first time, get under your skin. There is no more fascinating hobby than showing dogs. The bustle of the shows, the rush to get your dog ready, and the thrill of winning cannot be elsewhere equalled. To all this add lasting friendships built up through association with congenial companions met everywhere you exhibit, and you will appreciate why so many persons follow the shows with unrelenting interest, year after year.

A view of the benching area at the Detroit Kennel Club show. Benched shows are very rare today, but are the prime means the fancy and the interested public have of coming together. These are the show window of the dog fancy.

An interesting group: left to right, Mrs. C. C. Pacey (Wolvey), Mrs. D. P. Allom
(Furzefield), and Mr. E. A. Beels (O'Petriburg).

Mr. L. A. Haynes (Thornesian Kennels) with his Westie Working Pack, 1960s.

Post-War Activity in Britain

The breed suffered badly in Britain during the span of World War II. Shows were shut down completely and, with the exception of a few clandestine matches, there was no competitive action for six long years. Further, because of the bombings, the food shortage and the many more important personal considerations, those who had any dogs either boarded them in the country or drastically reduced the size of their kennels. These restrictive actions caused the fancy to fall away in both size and virility as the dog population dwindled.

With the coming of peace, the remaining enthusiasts re-grouped and quickly began to revive the spirit that had always made Britain great. It was not long before the initial post-war championship show in the breed was held in Peterborough in July of 1946 (Specialty of the West Highland White Terrier Club of England). Appropriately, the honor to judge fell upon the shoulders of Mrs. Winnie Barber, daughter of Holland Buckley. It was at this event that the first post-war Challenge Certificates were awarded and they went to the Hon. T. Rollo's Timochenko of the Roe (dog), and Charles Drake's Macairn's Jemima (bitch). Thereafter, show activity swelled rapidly and soon regained a large measure of its pre-war strength and enthusiasm.

The first Westies to gain their post-war titles were Mrs. J. Finch's (Shiningcliff) great dog, Eng. Ch. Shiningcliff Simon

195

Eng. Ch. Freshney Fiametta, owned by Mrs. E. E. Melville (Miss E. E. Wade).

Eng. Ch. Shiningcliff Sugar Plum

Four Wolvey champions of 1925.

(Eng. Ch. Leal Flurry ex Walney Thistle) and Miss E. E.
Wade's (Hookwood) fine bitch, Ch. Freshney Fiametta (Eng.
Ch. Melbourne Matthais ex Freshney Felicia). These two
breeders together with Dr. and Mrs. A. Russell (Cruben),
Mrs. D. M. Dennis (Branston), Mrs. M. McKinney (Freshney),
Miss M. Turnbull (Leal), Mr. and Mrs. Beels (O'Petriburg)
all aided strongly in the renassaince guided always by the steady-
ing influence of Mrs. C. C. Pacey.

Of this group, Mrs. Beels and Mrs. Dennis require special
mention. Mrs. Beels obtained her first Highlanders in 1924
from Miss Tufnell (Under the Steeple) and later purchased
Dude O'Petriburg from Mrs. Hewson's Clint Kennels. Dude
became the first of many champions to carry the O'Petriburg
suffix. Mrs. Beels was elected secretary of the West Highland
White Specialty Club (of England) in 1945 and held that important office almost continuously until 1964 when she became president, an office she resigned in 1971. Thus, Mrs.
Beels has had long contact with the breed and its fanciers and
is held in high esteem by all. Among her last champions were
Phelo and Phluster, both O'Petriburg. Mrs. Dennis also rates
special mention among the present-day group both for her
longevity of interest and success in the breed. Mr. and Mrs.
Dennis have been long-time fanciers reaching well before the
war and have bred and/or owned a host of toppers. Mrs. Dennis is possibly better known to American fanciers than most
because of the many successful show dogs that have come to
these shores through the years bearing the Branston name. Of
course, she is also widely known as the author of the English
treatise on the breed. At this writing she and Mr. Dennis continue to be active in both the club and the breed.

The British outlook has had its dark spots, however, and the
most depressing of these was the loss of Mrs. Pacey in the fall
of 1963. May Pacey was admittedly "the grand dame" of the
breed. Her name was synonymous with that of West Highland
White Terrier and well it should have been. She began breeding

197

operations before World War I and never in more than fifty years lost interest or enthusiasm. Her death is indeed an irreparable loss.

Mrs. Pacey's Wolvey Kennels bred and owned some 58 English titleholders, 40 of which she bred during its long tenure, and dogs bearing her prefix have been exported all over the world. The United States has been the main recipient with 23 U.S. Champions bearing the Wolvey stamp already on the rolls. Two of these have won Best in Show awards, Chs. Wolvey Pattern of Edgerstoune and Wolvey Pickwick.

Besides being an astute breeder (she also bred top flight Sealyham Terriers, Whippets and Greyhounds), Mrs. Pacey was a much sought after all-breed judge of international stature. She officiated the world over and at least twice to my memory judged at U.S. shows, the last time being in 1955 when she passed on the breed at the national specialty and then did additional Terriers and some Hound breeds at Westminster the following day.

At the conclusion of World War II she reactivated the West Highland White Terrier Club of England while rebuilding her badly depleted kennel and soon again was producing top Westies which she began exporting all over the world. In a very few years, Wolvey was as strong as ever and the entire breed benefited by her dedication. In fact, some 22 Wolvey dogs became champions during this period. Mrs. Pacey will live on in the memories of all who know her, and to those who did not, Wolvey will long be a name to remember.

In spite of the war and the loss of many fanciers through retirement or death over the years, British dogs are still prospering in the U.S. ring. Some of these dogs whose get have done well in this respect include Eng. Ch. Hookwood Mentor, sire of the great Ch. Cruben Dextor whose stud ability is documented elsewhere, is worthy of study. Mentor also sired among others mentioned, Eng. Ch. Barrister of Branston who in turn sired some 11 titleholders in Britain including two that became U.S. champions, namely, Bannoch of Branston and Slitrig Shandy. Barrister also sired two dogs that remained in

Eng. Ch. Barrister of Branston.

```
                                                    Eng. Ch. Wolvey Prefect
                                    Furzefield Provider
                                                    Eng. Ch. Placemore Prosperity
                    Furzefield Piper
                                                    Eng. Ch. Melbourne Mathias
                                    Furzefield Penelope
                                                    Furzefield Prunella
        Eng. Ch. Hookwood Mentor
                                                    Eng. Ch. Wolvey Prophet
                                    Brantvale Blinker
                                                    Belenoch
                    Bonchurch Bunty
                                                    Bonchurch Barman
                                    Bonchurch Babs
                                                    Furzefield Partisan
Eng. Ch. Barrister of Branston
                                                    Eng. Ch. Leal Flurry
                                    Eng. Ch. Melbourne Mathias
                                                    Leal Chieftainess
                    Brigadier of Branston
                                                    Freshney Andy
                                    Buzz of Branston
                                                    Baroness of Branston
        Bloom of Branston
                                                    Eng. Ch. Clint Cyrus
                                    Bobby of Branston
                                                    Blossom of Chemstone
                    Baroness of Branston
                                                    Eng. Ch. Clint Constable
                                    Belinda of Branston
                                                    Clint Coacla
```

199

Eng. Ch. Calluna the Poacher.

```
                                                        Eng. Ch. Calluna Ruaridh
                                      Eng. Ch. Leal Flurry
                                                        My Riviera Rose
                     Eng. Ch. Shiningcliff Simon
                                                        Eng. Ch. Wolvey Prefect
                                      Walney Thistle
                                                        White Sheen of Wick
          Calluna Bingo
                                                        Cruben Flash
                                      Ch. Cruben Cranny of Edgerstoune
                                                        Cruben Miss Seymour
                     Cruben Miss Rustle
                                                        Cruben Chief
                                      Cruben Oddity
                                                        Banrigh na Fhrasiche
Eng. Ch. Calluna the Poacher
                                                        Eng. Ch. Wolvey Prefect
                                      Furzefield Provider
                                                        Eng. Ch. Placemore Prosperity
                     Furzefield Piper
                                                        Eng. Ch. Melbourne Mathias
                                      Furzefield Penelope
                                                        Furzefield Prunella
          Calluna Vermintrude
                                                        Eng. Ch. Leal Flurry
                                      Eng. Ch. Melbourne Mathias
                                                        Leal Chieftainess
                     Calluna Nike
                                                        Closburn Clonnie
                                      Calluna Victory Wings
                                                        Calluna Carry On
```

200

England but which made their presence felt in America through their progeny. The first was the great Eng. Ch. Banker of Branston who is responsible for Ch. Bavena of Branston imported by Mrs. Mellon and Mrs. Keenan's memorable winner, Ch. Rainsborowe Redvers. Of course Banker also sired Eng. Ch. Bandsman of Branston who is a sterling English stud force and who will surely be heard from through his offspring. The second important stud sired by Barrister is Eng. Ch. Calluna Big Wig who fathered three U.S. titleholders in Chs. Wycote Bramhill Brocade, Phrana O'Petriburg and Cruben Happy. It is interesting to study the pedigree of Barrister which represents five generations of careful Branston breeding towards an ultimate goal. That this goal was reached is apparent from the record of 21 champions since the war.

Mrs. E. A. Beel's Eng. Ch. Calluna The Poacher, bred by Miss A. A. Wright, and a grandson of Eng. Ch. Shiningcliff Simon was a ten certificate winner during his long and fruitful ring career but his efforts at stud were even more noteworthy

Eng. Ch. Calluna The Laird.

Eng. Ch. Calluna the Laird	Ch. Laird of Lochalon	Eng. Ch. Rosalan Rogue	Eng. Ch. Hookwood Sensation → Eng. Ch. Hookwood Mentor / Eng. Ch. Freshney Fiametta
		Rosalan Regina	Furzefield Piper / Avonia Glamour Girl
	Susan of Northcliff	Eng. Ch. Barrister of Branston	Eng. Ch. Hookwood Mentor / Bloom of Branston
		Lucinda of Laurinar	Brigadier of Branston / Waltham Georgina
	Calluna Sheenagh	Calluna Gorbals Diehard	Calluna Bingo → Eng. Ch. Shiningcliff Simon / Cruben Miss Rustle
		Calluna Vermintrude	Furzefield Piper / Calluna Nike
	Calluna Sae Sonsie	Eng. Ch. Shiningcliff Simon	Eng. Ch. Leal Flurry / Walney Thistle
		Calluna Susan	Calluna Bingo / Calluna Vermintrude

201

Eng. Ch. Banker of Branston.

Eng. Ch. Sollershott Soloist.

Eng. Ch. Petriburg Mark of Polteana, a 1963 titlist.

since he sired at least six U.S. titleholders including Chs. Lochglen Jubilee Jill, Lochglen Haigus, Lochglen Lorrel, Tea Rose of Trenean, Phreesia O'Petriburg and Famecheck Viking. That Viking had "the Poacher's" blood in his veins was evident since both dogs were famed for their lasting qualities and both made startling ring appearances at about ten years of age.

Miss A. A. Wright bred another dog that is well represented by his U.S. progeny. This dog was Eng. Ch. Calluna The Laird. He gains his greatest fame through his illustrious son Ch. Elfinbrook Simon and in addition has sired Chs. Snowcliff Jeannie, Bee of Raventofts, Waideshouse Willow and Wish Me Luck, truly an imposing list. Many others have scored in the U.S. through their expatriated get, but those noted merit special attention since the pattern of success is apparent and the old adage, "like father—like son" was never nearer to the truth.

At this point, it may be well to list a few additional breeders who have more recently come into the spotlight through their efforts and dogs. Probably the most successful of these, so far as exports to the United States is concerned, is Miss F. M. C. Cook of Famecheck Kennels. She has exported some 34 Westies to this country that have completed their titles (through 1975). A few of the more noteworthy were: Chs. Famecheck Lucky Charm, Famecheck Viking, Famecheck Miranda, Famecheck Texan, Famecheck Romeo, Famecheck Platinum and Famecheck Busy Body. In England, Miss Cook has brought along some 25 titleholders since 1954 to offer a balanced output of quality dogs that cannot be overlooked.

Mrs. J. E. Beer's Whitebriar Kennels is another that has enjoyed very good fortune here with some 19 Highlanders bearing her prefix already gaining titles. These include the best in show winners Ch. Whitebriar Journeyman and the notable Ch. Whitebriar Jalisker. Mrs. D. J. Kenney-Taylor, while no longer active in the breed, had the good fortune to breed the Eng. Ch. Sollershott Soloist, who was very successful in England, circa 1964. She also bred Ch. Sollershott Sober who completed his English title and then came to the United States where he proved a consistent winner for about three years. The Quakertown Kennels of Mrs. H. Sansom has also done well on both

Eng. Ch. Quakertown Quistador,
owned by Mrs. K. Sansom.

Eng. Ch. Quakertown Querida,
owned by Mrs. K. Sansom.

204

sides of the water through the years. Eng. Ch. Quakertown Quistador was one of the leading winners in England during both 1964 and 1965 with a total of 16 challenge certificates including three specialty show "bests". He was sired by Eng. Ch. Alpin of Kendrum ex Eng. Ch. Quakertown Querida, a bitch that I will not soon forget since I saw her take her first CC at the National Terrier show in 1968. She looked and acted like a youngster and it was surprising to find that she had been whelped in 1960, nearly eight years before. Age seemed to make no difference as she finished during the same year to demonstrate again that the Highlander is always young at heart and generally ageless in actions. In this country the banner is upheld by the likes of Chs. Quakertown Quipette and Quakertown Quirang.

Mrs. S. J. Kearsey (Pillerton) is another breeder that has done extremely well with a long line of winning Highlanders. The best known of her dogs is unquestionably, Eng. Ch. Pillerton Peterman (Slitrig Simon ex Pillerton Pickle). A home-bred, he was an excellent winner during the years 1965–1967, capturing a total of nine challenge certificates. Overshadowing his ring prowess, however, is his prepotency as a stud force. To date, he has sired a long list of champions and in particular some five that have come to America that have gained best in show awards. These are, Chs. Pinmoney Puck, Lymehills Birkfell Solstice, Purston Pinmoney Pedlar, Pillerton Peterkin and Purston Polly Perkins. Another of Mrs. Kearsey's studs, Pillerton Perry, is the sire of Dr. Hunt's big winner, Ch. Highlands Angus. Of substantial interest, however, is the fact that Mrs. Kearsey is now in the United States, having come over in 1975 and has established residence here. Of course, she brought over many of her dogs, including Peterman. While the dog is along in years, there is small doubt that he will further improve the number of his successful get in America as he is in much demand as a stud.

At this point, it may be well to note that during her last seven or eight years in England, Mrs. Kearsey cooperated with Michael Collings (Purston) who, though he has had a relatively short sojourn in the breed, has an eye for a good

The two photographs on this page are both of a most remarkable dog. This is Eng. Ch. Pillerton Peterman (Slitrig Simon of Lynnwood ex Pillerton Pickle. The top photo shows him at 13 months and just starting on his successful show career. A prepotent sire in England, Peterman fathered no less than five American Best in show winners. In 1975 Peterman came to live in America with his owner-breeder, Sylvia J. Kearsey and at this writing is still siring at over twelve years. The lower photo shows him in December 1976, posing for his American portrait.

one. Further, he took full advantage of Peterman's prepotency and used the dog successfully while buying his get whenever possible. As a result, there are many fine dogs that carry the Purston prefix in both England and America. Of course, one of the very best is Ch. Purston Pinmoney Pedlar, one of the all-time top Highlanders in the American ring. Again, the name Ch. Purston Polly Perkins comes up while the recently retired winner, Ch. Ardenrun 'Andsome of Purston began his show career in England where he was finished by Collings and was the top West Highlander in 1973. A full list of Colling's dogs that have made good in England and/or in America would be long and revealing. Suffice it to say, he has bred and bought the best and has sent over a number of top winners.

Another strong breeder that is active both in breeding and exhibiting is Miss Sheilah Cleland. Success has been steady with a host of good dogs bearing her Birkfell prefix. Miss Cleland is known in the U.S., having judged over here, and through a number of good exports to America. In 1975 alone, three dogs bearing her prefix, Chs. Birkfell's Shepherd's Plaid, Sweet and Lovely and Shepherd's Dance did well in the American ring while many other Birkfell dogs will be discovered in both English and American records of the breed.

Another establishment of merit is the Estcoss Kennels of Mrs. V. L. W. Estcourt. It owned the consistent winner, Eng. Ch. Citrus Lochinvar of Estcoss (Eng. Ch. Sollershott Sun Up ex Famecheck Foxtrot), who has already sired three titlists. Mrs. Estcourt's Eng. Ch. Rhianfa Up and Coming of Estcoss was a notable winner and was best Terrier bitch at Crufts (1968). She is by Lochinvar ex Rhianfa Rainsborowe Poppea.

The working of Terriers is still a sport in England and The Sporting Terrier Association is a group that offers working action and competition for dogs originally propagated for such pursuits. At least one Westie enthusiast, L. A. Haynes of the Thornesian prefix, not only shows his Highlanders but also hunts them in a pack reminiscent of activities around the turn of

207

the century. An illustration of his pack is shown in this book, and it will be noted that the dogs travel together as in the past with the game uppermost in their minds. Mr. Haynes stock not only hunts but is capable of upholding its position in the show ring as well. They are shown at championship and sanction events and do well. In fact, Thornesian Coelogyne recently won best in show at the Leed's Sporting Terrier event held in early 1969.

Other breeders that deserve mention include: Mr. and Mrs. B. Thomson, of Waideshouse fame, who have sent over several good winners bearing their prefix, including the late Ch. Waideshouse Wiloughby; Mr. Len Pearson (Snowcliff) who has been instrumental in sending many good dogs to Mrs. Sayres, including Simon; Mrs. G. N. Barr, a long-time breeder and owner of the Stoneygap prefix; Mrs. A. M. Sager who has the Rhianfa Kennels; Mrs. Noel Whitworth, now deceased, of Raventofts fame; Mr. C. Berry and Mrs. B. Wheeler for the successful imports carrying the Incheril and Alpingay prefixes respectively. Additionally, a number of others have gained prominence during the past decade or so. Interestingly enough, two of this group have long been closely associated with the Scottish Terrier fancy. They are Miss Muriel Owen of Gaywyn fame and Mrs. Elizabeth Meyer of Rheanda. Both prefixes are becoming significant factors in the West Highland White Terrier ring. Also gaining position are such names as: C. Oakley and A. Shaw (Ardenrun); Mr. and Mrs. Lees (Carillyon); Mr. H. Davies (Clynebury); G. B. Painting (Finearte), breeder of the widely known Ch. Glengordon Fine-arte Prince of Peace (Ch. Sarmac Heathstream Drummer Boy ex Ch. Cedarfell Messenger Dove), now owned by Mrs. H. K. Budden (Glengordon); Miss A. Millen (Sarmac), owner of Ch. Sarmac Heathstream Drummer Boy (Ch. Lindenhall Drambui ex Heathstream Mistyfell), a dog bred by Mrs. Farnes (Heathstream) and top Westie in 1973. Drambui, in turn, is a son of the widely known Ch. Sollershott Soloist. J. W. Hodsall (Furzeleigh) is another strong exhibitor and

208

Eng. Ch. Citrus Lochinvar of Estcoss,
owned by Mrs. V. L. W. Estcourt.

Eng. Ch. Rhianfa Up and Coming of Estcoss,
owned by Mrs. V. L. W. Estcourt.

209

Ch. Dianthus Buttons, owned and bred by Mrs. K. Newstead, made history for the breed by winning best in show at Crufts in 1976. It was the first time a West Highland was named Supreme Champion at Britain's premier all-breed show. He is shown here in the presentation of terrier group first under Diana Hamilton (center) enroute to the top award. The handler is Geoffrey Corrish.

the present owner of the very successful stud force, Ch. White-briar Jonfair (Whitebriar Johncock ex Whitebriar Jeenay), bred by Mrs. Beer; Mr. D. Tattersall (Olac); Mr. and Mrs. K. Abbey (Kristajen); Mr. and Mrs. A. Bonas (Tasman); Mrs. Bertram (Highstile); Mrs. Coy (Cedarfell); Mrs. Graham (Lasara); Mrs. Taylor (Checkbar) and, of course, Mrs. K. Newstead of Appleton, Lancashire. Mrs. Newstead is the proud owner-breeder of Ch. Dianthus Buttons (Ch. Alpin of Kendrum ex Starcyl Sioux) a big winner in 1975 but Best in show at Crufts in 1976, an honor never before gained by a West Highlander. Of course, Button's triumph has done much to further popularize the breed around the world and as one who has seen the dog in the flesh, he was fully deserving of the honor. There are many, many more breeders and dogs that should be mentioned but space does not permit a more detailed index. Britain, like America, has a great influx of new talent that is breeding intelligently and with excellent results.

Since several British dogs have been so important to the propagation of the Highlander in America, four-generation pedigrees are offered for Eng. Chs. Barrister of Branston, Calluna The Poacher and Calluna The Laird. Also, information concerning all Westies that have become English titleholders is given together with a year-by-year listing of English Westie registrations which offers an interesting comparison with similar figures given for U.S. activities. It will be noted that although the British register substantial numbers of Westies every year, they complete championships on only about one-tenth as many dogs as we do.

It has been taken by some as a measure of overall quality whereby the British are believed to have better dogs across the board. This is not a fact, however. Having viewed many English shows, it appears to this writer that quality is much the same and that just as many entrants at English events are of only average quality. The difference is in the systems used in the two countries. In England, all champions must compete in the open classes whereby the opportunity for challenge certificates is lessened appreciably, especially when a top dog is in competition all year. Further, there are only about two dozen shows per year at which challenge certificates are offered. These rule differences hold down the number of champions quite drastically and few breeds have any great number being made up in any year. This, of course, is in direct contrast to the U.S., where championship points are available at every show. Thus, it is believed that an English champion must be of well above average quality to qualify while in this country, such is not the case. However, the average quality of the breed is little different.

It must be admitted that the British are staunch supporters of the breed and are more dedicated to it than many Americans. Few successful British breeders fall by the wayside after five or ten years of activity as they often do in the United States. In Britain it seems that once a Westie breeder, always a Westie breeder.

Before closing this chapter I would like to comment upon an additional point of interest. This deals with the use of the name "Westie" as a term for the breed. It is used frequently in this book and is a commonly heard term for the breed at dog shows and other gatherings. Its use has been criticized at times but little notice of these criticisms has been taken until I read that Mrs. Pacey did not think the name appropriate because "it sounds like something soft." Criticism by a person of her stature requires rebuttal and to this end I enlist the aid of Mrs. Anthony Walters's able pen, she being an authority on all things Scottish. Mrs. Walters, explaining the use of the name when it was subjected to similar criticism several years ago, wrote in the *American Kennel Gazette* as follows:

"Anyone knowing the Scot's dialect realizes that the 'ie' termination is one of affection and endearment rather than 'softness.' Burns calls his mouse, 'wee beastie' and many a 'dearie,' 'bairnie,' 'laddie' and 'lassie' slips from the lips of the Scot as he addresses his loved ones. A venerable and elderly Scottish surgeon whom I knew well as a child, invariably referred to his equally elderly and sedate wife as 'wee

212

Wifie.' So as long as we love and cherish our West Highland White Terriers, let them be 'Westies.' "

I think this dissertation properly evaluates the use of the term. It is not one of "softness" but rather one of affection and we all, I hope, love our Westies. Burns once wrote:

> "He was a gash an' faithful tyke,
> As ever lap a sleugh or dyke,
> His honest, sonsie, baws'nt face,
> Ay gat him friends in ilka place."

An apt description of the Highlander, or should I say the Westie.

Eng. Ch. Phelo O'Petriburg,
owned by Mrs. J. A. W. Beels.

West Highland White Terrier
ENGLISH KENNEL CLUB REGISTRATIONS
from 1907 to 1975

1907	141	1930	345	1953	895
1908	249	1931	261	1954	948
1909	351	1932	267	1955	1080
1910	442	1933	598	1956	1327
1911	583	1934	628	1957	1263
1912	596	1935	718	1958	1448
1913	631	1936	757	1959	1785
1914	522	1937	682	1960	2070
1915	239	1938	633	1961	2344
1916	193	1939	424	1962	2614
1917	97	1940	138	1963	2744
1918	55	1941	135	1964	2884
1919	126	1942	175	1965	3113
1920	244	1943	277	1966	3094
1921	371	1944	494	1967	3611
1922	499	1945	675	1968	4160
1923	587	1946	1017	1969	4837
1924	688	1947	1056	1970	4933
1925	372	1948	1114	1971	4097
1926	348	1949	1193	1972	4510
1927	327	1950	1018	1973	4472
1928	347	1951	992	1974	4630
1929	350	1952	968	1975	3913

ENGLISH CHAMPIONS
from 1907 to 1976

1907: Morven
Oransay
Cromar Snowflake
1909: Keltie
1910: Runag
Pure Gem
1911: Cairn Nevis
Lagavulin
1912: Cairn Ransa
Morova
Scotia Chief
Blantyre Minnie
Swaites Cruachan
1913: Kilree Bag O'Tricks
Rosalie of Childwick
1914: Lothian Defender
Moreso
Mountaineer
Glenmhor Guanag
Maulden Creena
1915: Hyskear of Childwick
Ornsay Defender
Repton Rollick
Chatty of Childwick
1916: Wolvey Piper
Wolvey Rhoda
1917-19: No Awards
(World War I)
1920: Charming of Childwick
Highclere Rhalet
Highclere Romp
White Sylph
Wolvey Skylark
1921: Chum of Childwick
Craig Witch
Highclere Roamer
1922: Barlae Perfection
Gwern Wilfred
Wolvey Chieftain
Wolvey Jean
Wolvey Perseus
1923: Gwern Remembrance
Harviestoun Mab
Highclere Rescuer

Maulden Miranda
Wolvey Fanny
Wolvey Vida
Wolvey Clover
1924: Chiel of Childwick
White Sylvia
Wolvey Guy
1925: Alpha of Gunthorpe
Crivoch Cadet
Culprit of Gunnersbury
Ornsay Sporran
White Smasher
Wolvey Witch
1926: Cooden Sapper
Cooden Suzanne
Crivoch Cheery
Furzefield Patience
Little Dusty
Wolvey Patrician
Wolvey Patron
1927: Cooden Swankpot
Crivoch Candida
Dornie Busybody
Gwern Dwynwen
Wolvey Patrol
Wolvey Wish
1928: Betsy MacPherson
Cooden Safety
Kilfinichen Kirsty
Moses of Daneend
Ophir Chiel
Ophir Nancy
1929: Carlin Melvich
Elmslea Reyna
Fidus Flos
Gay Lad of Alard
Leal Heatherbell
Ophir Rowdy
Placemore Caution
Ray of Rushmoor
Rita of Rushmoor
1930: Cooden Shrapnel
Cooden Stonechat
Ruth of Rushmoor

215

Wolvey Pauline
Wolvey Pepper
1931: Clint Cocktail
Cooden Steeplechaser
Cooden Sunita
Major's Mite of Dane's End
Reba Romance
Rodrick of Rushmoor
Rooney of Rushmoor
1932: Clint Cheek
Columbine Cariad
Cooden Skypilot
Dante of Dane's End
Placemore Prosperity
Skelum of the Roe
Wings
1933: Bobby Bingo
Brean Taurie
Carlin Rose
Clint Topper
Leeside Larkspur
Wolvey Poacher
Wolvey Primrose
1934: Brean Glunyieman
Columbine Cilean
Cooden Sheena
Dude O'Petriburg
Gwili Glendid
Leal Patricia
Wolvey Peacock
1935: Brean Skelpie
Calluna Clos
Clint Chief
Jenifer
Leal Phoenix
Wolvey Pandora
Wolvey Poet
1936: Brean Lonnie
Clint Constable
Rowenna of Rushmoor
Wolvey Pintail
Wolvey Pongo
Wolvey Prefect
1937: Brean Gluclos
Calluna Ruairidh
Clint Cyrus
Columbine Cumanta
Throxenby Tempest
Wolvey Prophet

1938: Brean De Berri
Corrichie Cillmargo
Leal Flurry
Leal Sterling
MacEwan's Gift
Misterdawson
Walfield Margaret
Wolvey Pattern
Wolvey Phantom
Wolvey Plainsman
Wolvey Playfellow
1939: MacSporran of Tiriosal
Melbourn Mathias
Robina of Rushmoor
Rowberrow Rapture
Rowson of Rushmoor
1940-46: No Awards
(World War II)
1947: Betty of Whitehills
Freshney Fiametta
Shiningcliff Simon
Timoshenko of the Roe
1948: Baffle of Branston
Pygmalion of Patterscourt
Hookwood Mentor
Deidre of Kendrum
Cruben Crystal
Macairns Jemina
Wolvey Prospect
1949: Athos of Whitehills
Binnie of Branston
Furzefield Pax
Heathcolne Freshney Flare
Lorne Jock
Macconachie Tiena Joy
Shiningcliff Storm
Wolvey Penelope
Wolvey Prudence
1950: Barrister of Branston
Brisk of Branston
Furzefield Preference
Heathcolne Roamer
Isla of Kendrum
Maree of Kendrum
Shiningcliff Sprig
1951: Cruben Dextor
Crystone Chatterer
Crystone Cherry
Furzefield Provost

216

Ch. Alpinegay Sonata.

Ch. Lorell Last Legacy.

Ch. Carillyon Cadence.

Ch. Cedarfell Merry 'N Bright.

Ch. Glengordon Hannah.

Ch. Checkbar Donsie Kythe.

Hookwood Sensation
Lynwood Branston Blue
Mallaig Silver Empress
Mark of Old Trooper
Shiningcliff Snowcloud
Shiningcliff Sultan
Staplands Shepherd
1952: Cotsmor Crunch
Furzefield Pilgrim
Hasty Bits
Heathcolne Gowan
Perchance of Patterscourt
Shiningcliff Dunthorne
  Damsel
Staplands Spitfire
Wolvey Piquet
Wolvey Poster
1953: Calluna The Poacher
Cotsmor Cream Puff
Cruben Moray
Hookwood Gardenia
Lynwood Blue Betty
Lynwood Timothy
Rosalan Rogue
Shiningcliff Donark Decision
Shiningcliff Sugar Plum
Wolvey Peach
Wolvey Poppet
1954: Bannock of Branston
Biretta of Branston
Cotsmor Creambun
Eoghan of Kendrum
Famecheck Lucky Charm
Laird of Lochalan
Mairi of Kendrum
Tulyar of Trenean
Wolvey Pageboy
1955: Brendalee
Famecheck Viking
Lynwood Marcia
Nice Fella of Wynsolot
Quakertown Quality
Raventofts Fuchsia
Rowmore Brora of Kennishead
Slitrig Solitaire
1956: Banda of Branston
Bramhill Patricia
Famecheck Gay Crusader
Famecheck Happy Knight

Slitrig Shandy
Wolvey Patricia
Wolvey Philippa
Wolvey Pied Piper
1957: Banker of Branston
Cruben Chilibean
Crystone Cressina
Famecheck Ballet Dancer
Famecheck Comet
Famecheck Lucky Mascot
Kirnbrae Symmetra Sailaway
Mistymoor Andrea
Wolvey Pirate
1958: Brindie of Branston
Calluna the Laird
Famecheck Gaiety Girl
Famecheck Lucky Choice
Famecheck Lucky Roger
Freshney Frey
Quakertown Questionnaire
Rivelin Rustle
Shiningcliff Sheela
Sollershot Sun Up
Stoneygap Commodore
Wolvey Pipers Son
Wolvey Postmaster
1959: Banessa of Branston
Bavena of Branston
Broomlaw Brandy
Citrus Warbler
Cruben Happy
Eriegael Mercedes
Famecheck Jolly Warrior
Furzefield Patrick
Phrana O'Petriburg
Wolvey Palor
Wolvey Pipers Tune
Wolvey Postgirl
1960: Bandsman of Branston
Broomheather Freesia
Eriegael Storm Child
Famecheck Gay Buccaneer
Famecheck Joy
Famecheck Musketeer
Glengyle Tapestry
Stoneygap Flash
Symmetra Skirmish
Wolvey Pavlova
Wolvey Playgirl

219

Ch. Whitebriar Jonfair, owned by J. W. Hodsall and bred by Mrs. J. E. Beer, stands out as a noteworhy winner and producer. He was reserve best terrier at Crufts 1975 to the eventual BIS winner, but is probably most familiar to American fanciers as the sire of Dr. Alvaro T. Hunt's Ch. Ardenrun Andsome of Purston.

Ch. Sarmac Heathstream Drummer Boy, owned by Mrs. Audrey Millen, was one of Britain's top winners in the early 1970s. A winner of 12 CCs, he is also a successful sire.

Workman of Wynsolot
1961: Brenda of Branston
Broomheather Fleur de Lis
Buttons of Helmleigh
Glengyle Thistle
Phancy O'Petriburg
The Prior of Raventofts
Wolvey Permit
Wolvey Pickwick
1962: Alpin of Kendrum
Banner of Branston
Banny of Branston
Birkfell Sea Shanty
Birkfell Solitaire
Famecheck Madcap
Slitrig Sachet
Sollershot Soloist
Stoneygap Bobbin of Gillobar
Wolvey Punch
1963: Billybong of Branston
Busybody of Branston
Lasara Lee
Petriburg Mark of Polteana
Slitridge Shiningstar
of Lynwood
Sollershot Symphony
Stoneygap Sugar Candy of
Mahnraf
Waideshouse Woodpecker
Whitebriar Jimolo
Wolvey Paperman
1964: Baggage of Branston
Citrus Lochinvar of Estcoss
Kandymint of Carryduff
Mahgni Wooster
Quakertown Quistador
Rhianfa Rifleman
Rivelin Rhumba
Snowcliff Springsong
Waideshouse Warrant
Waideshouse Woodlark
1965: Bardel of Branston
Briarrose of Branston
Glengyle Teasle
Phelo O'Petriburg
Phluster O'Petriburg
Pillerton Pippa
Sollershot Freshney Foy
Sollershot Sober

1966: Alpingay Impressario
Birkfell Summer Sun
Famecheck Verona
Glengyle Blakpoynt White Magic
Incheril Amaryllis
Monsieur Aus der Flerlage
Pillerton Peta
Pillerton Peterman
Waideshouse Willoughby
1967: Birkfell Sea Fire
Famecheck Bernard
Famecheck Dainty Maid
Famecheck Hallmark
Glengyle Trade
Highstile Poppet
Highstile Prank
Lasara Louise
MacNab of Balmaha
Masquerade of Bamburgh
Morenish Geordie
Pinkholme Paramount
Slitridge Go Shell of Branston
Snow Goblin
Strathairlie Swiss Miss
Woodpuddle Bawbee
Woodpuddle Bumble
1968: Alpingay Sonata
Famecheck Maid To Order
Famecheck Trojan
Glengyle Tuggles
Lindenhall Discord
Quakertown Querida
Renlim Rachel
Rhianfa Up and Coming
of Estcoss
Waideshouse Waterboy
Whitebriar Jillian
1969: Birkfell Solace
Birkfell Solitude
Checkbar Donsie Kythe
Checkbar Remony Rye
Famecheck Fashionplate
Famecheck Sterling
Glengyle Taiho
Highstile Priceless
Lindenhall Donna
Lindenhall Drambuie
Lorell Last Legacy
Quakertown Quandry

221

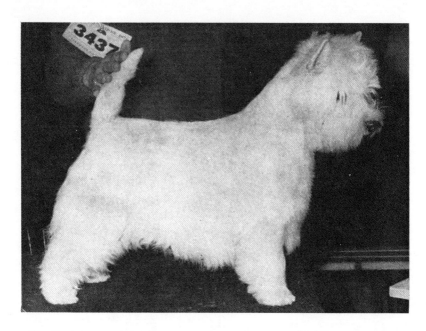

Ch. Pillerton Prejudice, owned by Sylvia J. Kearsey and bred by Rev. Collings, a national specialty show winner in England.

Ch. Birkfell Silver Thistle of Clanestar, owned by Mrs. D. K. Lancaster and bred by Miss Sheila Cleland.

1970: Heath of Backmuir
Rosyles Promise
Thornesian Marquis
Cedarfell Messenger Dove
Famecheck Air Hostess
Sumar Glengidge Tucket
1971: Checkbar Tommy Quite Right
Bradbury of Branston
Incheril Inge
Ballacoar Musette of
Cedarfell
Famecheck Grannis
Sealaw Selena
Pillerton Peterkin
Highstyle Phidget
Cedarfell Merry N'Bright
Whitebriar Jonfair
1972: Sarmac Heathstream Drum-
mer Boy
Rhianfa Take Notice
Medallist of Cedarfell
Birkfell Sea Squall
Tasman March on Time
Melwyn Pillerton Picture
Birkfell Solicitude
Tasman Adoration
Famecheck Busybody
Lasara Limpet
White Rose of Ide
1973: Ardenrun Andsome of
Purston
Clantartan Chrysanthemum
Commander of Tintibar
Cedarfell Moon Melody
Drumcope Dewdrop
Easter Bonnetina
Gaywyn Brandy of
Branston

Gaywyn Gypsy
Glengordon Finearte
Prince of Peace
Halfmerek Marina
Lasara Linda Belle
Nailbourne Nutcracker
Pillerton Prejudice
Purston Petite
1974: Birkfell Soliloquy
Checkbar Findlay McDougal
Milburn Mandy
Dianthus Buttons
Furzeleigh Last Edition
Olac Moonraker
Famecheck Silver Charm
Birkfell Silver Thistle
of Clanestar
Purston Peter Pan
Erisort Special Edition
Drumcope Teddy Tar
Lucky of Loughore
1975: Robbie McGregor of Wyther Park
Binate Inverary
Glenalwyne Sonny Boy
Incheril At Large
Carillyon Cadence
Melwyn Milly Molly Mandy
Candida of Crinan
Ballacoar Samantha
Yelrav Spangle
Glengordon Hanaah
Justrite Jacinda
1976: Olac Moonbeam
Birkfell Snowbird
Kirkgordon Musical Cowboy
Meryt Silver Secret
Backmuir Noble James
Ashgate Lochinvar

223

"With no small amount of self-esteem" the West Highland equally distinguishes himself as a peerless show dog, a courageous earth dog and a most endearing companion. To those who know the breed best, it is no surprise that he is so well-regarded at the present time.

Breed Information

The growth of interest in purebred dogs during the past 25 years has been phenomenal, and the added attention given to the West Highlander during the same period has shown a similar expansive trend. This trend is worth studying briefly in order to understand the rather significant changes that are taking place every year in the dog fancy.

Looking over the long history of purebred dogs, we find that the first dog registered in *The American Kennel Club Stud Book* was an English Setter, "Adonis," owned by George Delano of New Bedford, Massachusetts. This occurred in 1878 and marked the beginning of an activity that has met with favor as a hobby, a business, and a pleasure. It grew slowly at first and then, as time passed, progressed with increasing rapidity. It took 57 years before the first million purebreds were entered into the rolls of the studbook and 1935 was the year. The second million took much less time, only ten years, and the goal was reached in 1945. The next ten years marked a tremendous growth, with another three million registered. Today the figure is astronomical. The current registrations rate is about one million a year. Is it any wonder that persons who follow these trends predict untold progress in dogs during the coming years?

While purebred dogs have been gaining in popularity, our Highlander has been doing very well. Complete figures are not available, but a listing of registrations since 1928 reflects a steady upswing except during the war years. These figures are shown on the placement of the Westies among all breeds for each year where available. These statistics show that the Westie has gained ground consistently and has shown exceptional improvement since 1961.

West Highland White Terrier
AMERICAN KENNEL CLUB REGISTRATIONS
from 1928 to 1976

1928	–	60		1952	–	354 (48)
1929	–	49		1953	–	423 (46)
1930	–	80		1955	–	458 (47)
1931	–	69 (39)		1956	–	529 (45)
1932	–	86 (35)		1957	–	599 (45)
1933	–	77 (41)		1958	–	605 (45)
1934	–	92 (41)		1959	–	667 (46)
1935	–	184 (38)		1960	–	625 (45)
1936	–	183 (39)		1961	–	699 (44)
1937	–	148 (44)		1962	–	930 (39)
1938	–	148 (44)		1963	–	1136 (39)
1939	–	175 (41)		1964	–	1409 (39)
1940	–	179 (43)		1965	–	1957 (39)
1941	–	120 (52)		1966	–	2560 (35)
1942	–	132 (50)		1967	–	3318 (35)
1943	–	103 (51)		1968	–	4057 (33)
1944	–	95 (49)		1969	–	4848 (35)
1945	–	134 (55)		1970	–	5801 (39)
1946	–	193 (56)		1971	–	6754 (38)
1947	–	232 (53)		1972	–	6577 (39)
1948	–	227 (54)		1973	–	6433 (41)
1949	–	240 (51)		1974	–	6493 (40)
1950	–	270 (50)		1975	–	5923 (40)
1951	–	324 (49)		1976	–	6071 (42)

( ) *Indicates rank among all breeds for year shown*

Kennel Identifications

When studying pedigrees, reading books, or listening to breed discussions, the names of various kennels are often noted or mentioned. Many of these are not known to the average person and some have been out of existence for many years and frequently evade identification. Added to these difficulties is the fact that so many dogs come from England that the country of derivation is often unknown. To aid the serious student of the breed to identify the several kennels as to owner and country the following listing is given. This is obviously not complete but it does designate many of the better known kennels in the United States, Great Britain, and Canada, together with the owner's name.

BRITISH KENNELS
(Past and Present)

ALPINGAY	Mrs. B. Wheeler
ARDENRUN	C. Oakley and A. Shaw
AVONIA	Mrs. F. Carter
BACKMUIR	Mr. and Mrs. A. Gellan
BALLACOAR	Mrs. S. Morgan
BIRKFELL	Miss S. Cleland
BLAKPOYNT	A. P. Reice
BONCHURCH	A. Brown
BRAMHILL	Mrs. J. M. Gee
BRANSTON	Mrs. D. M. Dennis
BREAN	Mrs. E. O. Innes
BUSHYMEADE	Miss F. E. Tuttle
CALLUNA	Miss A. Wright
CARILLYON	Mr. and Mrs. T. M. Lees
CEDARFELL	Mrs. M. P. Coy
CHECKBAR	Mrs. J. and Miss L. Taylor
CHILDWICK	Miss Vicars
CLANTARTAN	Miss J. E. Blakey
CLINT	Mrs. B. Hewson
CLONMEL	Holland Buckley
CLYNEBURY	Mr. H. Davies
COLUMBINE	Miss E. Shaw
COODEN	Capt. and Mrs. O. R. Williams
CRAIGMOOR	Mrs. E. Dickinson
CRINAN	Mrs. Barbara Hands

CRIVOCH .... Mrs. C. H. Smith
CRUBEN .... Dr. and Mrs. A. Russell
CULBAHN .... J. R. Jackson (Ireland)
DEANCOURT .... Miss P. Trotter
DIANTHUS .... Mrs. K. Newstead
DONARK .... Mrs. Dwyer
DUNBAR .... Mrs. D. K. Lancaster
ERISKAY .... A. Gillies
ESTCOSS .... Mrs. V. L. W. Estcourt
FAMECHECK .... Miss F. M. C. Cook
FINEARTE .... Mrs. G. B. Painting
FRESHNEY .... Mrs. M. McKinney
FURZEFIELD .... Mrs. D. P. Allom
FURZELEIGH ...... J. W. Hodsall
GAYWYN .... Miss C. Owen
GLENALWYNE ..... Miss J. Herbert
GLENGORDON ..... Mrs. H. K. Budden
GLENGYLE .... Mrs. P. M. Welch
GWERN .... Mrs. E. H. Spottiswoode and Miss Tufnel
HARVIESTOUN ..... Mrs. J. E. Kerr
HEATHCOLNE ..... Mrs. M. N. Baxter
HEATHSTREAM .... Mrs. J. Farnes
HIGHCLERE .... Mr. and Mrs. B. Lucas
HIGHSTILE .... Mr. and Mrs. T. Bertram
HOOKWOOD .... Miss E. E. Wade
INCHERIL .... C. Berry
INVERAILORT ..... Mr. and Mrs. Cameron-Head
KENDRUM .... Hon. T. H. Rollo
KENNISHEAD ...... Mrs. D. E. Wintergill
KRISTAJEN .... Mr. and Mrs. K. Abbey
LASARA .... Mrs. Graham and Mrs. Hazell
LEAL .... Miss M. Turnbull
LORELL .... Mrs. M. Duell
LYMEHILLS .... Mrs. L. V. Morton
MAHNRAF .... Mrs. D. Farnham
MALLAIG .... Mr. and Mrs. E. Bagshaw
MELPHIS .... Mr. and Mrs. E. Mellows
MELWYN .... Mrs. R. B. Pritchards
MHEALL .... J. Wills
MORENISH .... Miss E. C. Grieve
NEWTONGLEN ..... Mrs. T. A. Torbet
'OF THE ROE ...... Mrs. E. M. Garnett (Ireland)
O'PETRIBURG ...... Mrs. E. A. Beels
OPHIR .... Mr. and Mrs. A. J. Warren
ORNSAY .... J. Campbell

228

PATTERSCOURT ... W. J. Patterson
PILLERTON .... Mrs. S. J. Kearsey
PLACEMORE .... Mrs. C. M. Bird
POLTALLOCH ...... Col. E. D. Malcolm
PROKLEE .... Mrs. K. Proctor
PURSTON .... Michael Collings
QUAKERTOWN .... Mrs. H. Sansom
RAINSBOROWE .... Mrs. M. E. Pratten
RANROU .... Mrs. M. P. Fenlon
RAVENTOFTS ...... Mrs. Noel Whitworth
REANDA .... Mrs. E. Meyer
RIVELIN .... Mrs. M. W. Pearson
RENLIM .... Mr. and Mrs. W. H. Milner
RHIANFA .... Mrs. A. M. Sager
ROWBERROW ...... Mrs. F. Thornton
RUSHMOOR .... Miss V. M. Smith-Woods
SARMAC .... Mrs. Audrey Millen
SHININGCLIFF ..... Mrs. J. Finch
SLITRIG .... Mrs. C. M. Kirby
SNOWCLIFF .... Mr. and Mrs. A. Berry and Len Pearson
SOLLERSHOTT ..... Mrs. D. J. Kenney-Taylor
STONEYGAP .... Mrs. G. M. Barr
SURMAR .... Miss S. M. Jackson
SYMMETRA .... Mrs. J. Taylor
TASMAN .... Mr. and Mrs. A. Bonas
TAYBANK .... H. Ferrier
THORNESIAN ...... L. A. Haynes
TRENEAN .... Mrs. W. Dodgson
UNDER THE
  STEEPLE .... Miss Tufnell
WAIDESHOUSE ..... B. Thomson
WARBERRY .... Mrs. M. F. Hoyle
WHITEBRIAR ...... Mrs. J. E. Beer
WHITEBEAM .... Hon. Sybil Hood
WHITEHILLS ...... Mrs. V. M. Swann
WOLVEY .... Mrs. C. C. Pacey
WOODPUDDLE ..... Mrs. C. Ingram
WYNSOLOT .... Mrs. E. A. Green

UNITED STATES KENNELS
(Past and Present)

ACREAGE	Mrs. R. H. Gustin
BATTISON	Mr. and Mrs. Edward Danks
BAYOU GLEN	Dr. A. T. Hunt
BILJONBLUE	William Ferrara and John Price
BIRCHWOOD	Miss Dorothy Hardcastle
BELMERTLE	Dr. D. A. Tyler
BLAK-N-WITE	Cecil A. Dingman
BONNIE BRIER	Christine Swingle
BRIARCLIFF	Janet E. Lindgren
BRIARWOOD	B. King and B. Langdon
BYLINE	Mr. and Mrs. H. Pettis
CAIRNVRECKAN	Miss Amy Bacon
CHARAN	Capt. H. E. H. Chipman
CLAIREDALE	Mrs. C. Dixon
CLARKCREST	David Ogg and Dick Clark
CONEJO	Mrs. Roy Rainey
CRAGGENCROFT	Karen Lindberg
CRANBOURNE	Mr. and Mrs. John T. Marvin
D AND D	D. and D. Hanna
DE-GO	Dean Hughes
DEW WEST	Georgia DeWitt
DONNYBROOK	Mr. and Mrs. John T. Ward
DOON MCDUFF	Mr. and Mrs. J. W. Williams, Jr.
DORHILL	Mrs. Dorothy Hillner
DUKENDORF	D. and C. Rouse
EDGERSTOUNE	Mrs. John G. Winant
ELMVIEW	Mrs. L. L. Slygh
ELSINORE	Linda J. Servin
ENDCLIFFE	George Thomas
FLOGAN	Florise Hogan
FOREST GLEN	Mr. and Mrs. C. C. Fawcett
GAYTYKE	Mr. and Mrs. Roger E. Bell
GLENBRIAR	Mr. and Mrs. N. Stoll
GLENHAVEN	Miss L. Sutherland
GLENGIDGE	Mr. and Mrs. Seymour N. Weiss
GLENSHAR	Mr. and Mrs. Donald Frederick
GREENTREE	Mrs. Payne Whitney
HALO'S	Susan Napady
HAPPYMAC	B. and D. Mocabee
HEATHER HILL	Mrs. William Dexter
HEATHER-TYKE	Mrs. Donna Donovan

230

HERITAGE FARM ..	Shirley Jean O'Neill
HUNTINGHOUSE ..	Miss Katherine Hayward
ILLLENID'S	Mrs. Frank E. Dinelli
INVERARY	Perry Chadwick
JENESSEY	Mr. and Mrs. Ron Davis
JEROJET	Mr. and Mrs. J. Mecera
JOLEN'S	Mr. and Mrs. J. E. Craigmiles, Jr
KAR-RIC'S	Mrs. Doris Eisenberg
KENNELOT	L. M. Wood
KENWEST	Miss Harriet Kugler
KIRKALDY	Mrs. Robert Goddard
KIRK O'THE GLEN .	F. and P. Sherman
KLINTILLOCH	Mrs. S. M. Blue and Miss M. Williams
LAWRENTON	Mrs. J. E. Haskell
LOCH CREST	Mrs. Ruth Birmingham
LOCHGLEN	Mrs. Willard Boston
LONSDALE	Mr. and Mrs. J. Storey
MAC-A-DAC	Mrs. E. P. McCarty
MAC-KEN-CHAR	Mrs. Joanne Glodek
MAR-GRIN	Mrs. Harry Grindle
MARJEN	Mrs. M. Jensen
MAXWELTON	Mr. and Mrs. R. Lowry
MERRYHART	N. and J. Eberhardt
NATOS	Elaine Gnatowsky
NIC MAC	C. W. Lewis
NISHKENON	Mr. and Mrs. W. B. Rogers
NORWESTIE'S	M. and P. McAndrews
O'THE RIDGE	Marjadele Schiele
PENNYWORTH	Mrs. Peggy Newcombe
PROSSWICK	R. and M. Pross
RACHELWOOD	Mrs. R. K. Mellon
RANNOCH DUNE ..	Mrs. Frank Brumby
ROBINRIDGE	Mrs. A. S. Monroney
ROTHMORE	Mr. and Mrs. D. McKay-Smith
ROSSTOR	Miss Claudia Phelps
ROYAL TARTAN ..	R. and J. Hilliker
RUDH'RE	Joan Graber
SCOTCHBLOOM	Ms. Almary Henderson
SEE-ARE	Charles Ruggles
SEVENTH HEAVEN .	Mrs. Ruth Murgatroyd
SHIPTON	Mrs. E. Spencer
SINALCO	Mrs. G. F. Church
SKAKET'S	N. and E. Gauthier
SPRINGMEADE	Miss M. Van Schaick
SWEET BRIAR	Mrs. R. E. Preston
SUN CREST	Beverly Sundin

TRISKETT'S	Mrs. J. Vogelius
TYNDRUM	Mrs. A. Walters
VIMY RIDGE	Clifford Hallmark
WALLMOORE	Mrs. R. M. Cust
WARBONNET	M. and B. Hill
WESPRIDE	H. and J. Kellerman
WESTHERSIDE	Mrs. Constance C. Jones
WHIPSTICK	M. Evans and E. Rogers
WHITE OAKS	Dr., Mrs. and Laura Meisels
WHYTEHAVEN	Mr. and Mrs. Samuel Faust
WIGMAC	Mrs. Frame and Mrs. McCarty
WICKEN	Darlene Gralewicz
WIGTOWN	Mrs. B. G. Frame
WILOGLEN	Mr. and Mrs. A. Kotlisky
WIND CREST	P. and E. Haas
WINDRUSH	L. S. Penland
WISHING WELL	Mrs. Barbara Worcester Keenan
WOODLAWN	Mr. and Mrs. James Finley
WYNDERGAEL	Diane M. Fronczak

CANADIAN KENNELS

AVALON	Mrs. Pat Cook
BEN BRAGGIE	Fred Fraser
BENBULBEN	Mr. and Mrs. J. F. Crowe
BENCRUACHAN	Victor Blochin
CAVERNMOOR	Mr. and Mrs. Garry Gray
CLOCHNABEN	Mr. and Mrs. M. McGillivray
CROMARTY	Mr. and Mrs. Lorne Gignac
CRAIGSIDE	Ian Petrie
DELMANOR	D. and G. Collins
DREAMLAND	Mrs. A. A. Kaye
HARRIDALE	Mrs. L. J. Sherman
HEATHERBELLE ...	Mr. and Mrs. H. W. Mellish
HIGHLAND	Miss R. Billett and Miss Edith Humby
JOKAR'S	Mr. and Mrs. J. Liberman
JOLLIE'S	Mrs. Judie Crawford
LAURIE'S	Leonard Hunter
MANDERLEY	H. T. Flanagan
MACMOR	James Scott
'O THE LOCH	Mr. and Mrs. L. S. Frame
'OF THE ROUGE ...	Mrs. J. H. Daniell-Jenkins
REMASAIS	Mrs. M. Freemantle
ROSENEATH	Mrs. Thelma Adams
SALLYDEAN	Mrs. Sally Bremner
SHAGLE	G. and D. Thubron
SHIPMATES	Mrs. S. J. Navin
STOWE	D. and H. Seabrooke
THORNHILL	Mrs. H. C. LeFroy
WESTVALES	Mrs. Joan Carter
WINDE MERE	Mrs. Keith Balsdon

American Champions
1970 through 1976

Breed quality has more than kept up with the annual increase in registrations. Each year has shown a numerical improvement in champions finished and recently these figures have rivaled many breeds where the total number of registrations is many times that of the Highlander. The listings to follow do not necessarily mean that the dog completed its championship during the year noted but merely that its name was carried by the *American Kennel Gazette* during that year. The same is true of obedience winners.

A scene at the 1956 Morris & Essex show. Left to right: Ch. Wishing Well's High Tide (handled by Clifford Hallmark), Ch. Cruben Moray of Clairedale (Bob Gorman) and Ch. Tulyar of Trenean (Miss Barbara Worcester).

233

1970

Bonnie Brier Bilbo Baggins
Briarwood Bonnet
Dancing Hannah of the Rouge
Donnybrook's Jeffrey
Lo-Mar's Proud Texan
The Abominable Snowball
Westiewite's Dextor Flashback
Wigton Geraldine
Bryson's Blackgold Tornada
Donnybrook's Murphy
High Feather Becky
Klintilloch Monroe
Lochglen Kiltie
Nic-Macs Miss Stardust
Perk's Lad O'Balgownie
Pillerton Prosper
Wishing Well Wisp O'Buff Creek
Famecheck Fashionplate
Jerojet's Majorette
McCallion's Spur of the Moment
Purston Pinmoney Pedlar
Sou'westie Samantha
Thornemore Danelea Dawn
Winetta Winkle
De-Go Yulejock
Gairloch Amanda
Donnybrook's Jennifer
Ian of Lochalsh
Royal Tartan Kilt O'The Ridge
Winetta Warbaron
Wishing Well Quip O'Buff Creek
Woodlawn Copyright
Angus Macintish
Bargo of Branston
Famecheck Topmark
Farissier's Frosty Freddie
Impresario's Concert Master
Maxwelton First Fiddle
Purston Precocious
Sandoone Surprise
White Oaks Christmas Present
Ballantine Lucky Phillips

Byline Bob O'Branston
Flogan Flora
Flogan Fox Fire
Nic-Macs Mister Michael
Procne Penny
Rannoch-Dune Defiance Again
Royal Tartan Mac Bruce
Westwick's Sticky Wicket
Wigtown Daisy Mae
Barr's P Prentice
Famecheck Super Silver
Kar Ric's Absolutely Adorable
Mar-Grin's Cuileann Machielan
Nic-Mac's Call Girl
Rovel's Sassy Sally
Simon Sez Play Rugby
Whitebriar Jackfish
Bonnie Brier She's Groovin'
Crest-O-Lake Tough Guy
Headwood Drummer Boy
Kemp's Jig Lenox of Red Lodge
Lo-Mar's Thunder Cloud
Purston Peterson
Toyoko's Ichi Ban
Westcote Ghillie of Gairloch
Brigette of Mac-Ken-Char
Craggencroft Sir Andrew
Highland's Sampson
Jensemi Sergeant Pepper
Loch Crest Lady Caroline
MacDuff of Hillen-Dale
Mac Mahon's Miss Sweden
Azureglaen Devon Lancelot
Carus Edie
Dannyquest Warlock
Flogan Flame N Frost
Kris-Wils White Knight
Broon's Loch Ness Monster
Brytwood Gidget
Craggencroft Cuddihy, CD
Jenessey Paradox O'Peter Pan
Kar Ric's County Cork
Nichael's Wee Lad O'Arlwyn
Sno-Bilt's Lobil's Abby

Sno-Bilt's Raggedee Ann
Wiloglen's White Mist

1971

Bo-Mars Buffy Son of Duncan
Carroll's Heidi
Galworth's Scotch on the Rocks
Heritage Farm's Ode to Simon
Lo Mar's Corby Dukendorf
Nic-Macs Marquis
Alpingay Waltztime
Dannyquest Something Else
Dunweg Lady McBeth
Keepit of Dorhill
Keithall Marksman
Loch Crest Lealee
Ollieann's Little Roc
Rainbow Cicero
Snowcliff Morenish Eoghan
Tweed Teena-O-Donnybrook
Zipperer's Keg O'Dynamite
Impresario's Jerojet Musette
Rosyles Pirate
Stott's Majestic Atta Boy Dee
Sugarfrost White Shadow
Tervin Pixie
Winde Mere Gay Gordon
Woodlawn's Duncan
Brandy of Windy Hill
Coraland Bermudaful
Dreamland's Snowflake
Kenbrook Wee Thistle
Loch Crest Simon's Legacy
McTavish of Frosty Moor
McTwiddles Twiddle Dee
Purston Penelope
Reanda Magic Moment
Sun Crest Ginger Bread Man
Torvjord Peter Pumpkin Eater
Weaver's Highland Nugget
Winsom Lolita
Wishing Well's Happy Heart
Acreages Billy Bold

Impresario's Carousel
Lochinmar's Hot Toddy
Rollingwood's Apache Belle
Rollingwood's Aristocrat
Arlwyn Susie Q
Broadbridge Bearer
Castledoon's Tinker Toy
Kar Ric's Extra Edition
Kenbrook's Biz
Rannoch-Dune Diogenes
Sno-Bilt's Aquarius
Tartan's Pride and Joy
Wigtown Jassmine
Continental's Barby Doll
Dannyquest Too Much
Jaudon's De-Go Hussy
Pine's Beloved
Weaver's Highland Roxie
Allegro Banchee Brigadoon
Dannyquest Luci of Whytdale
Donnybrook's Ned
Ed Sun's Airy Little Rascal
Jolen's Lisa Mingon
Jolen's Viki Fiona
Kirk O'The Glen's Camelot
Weaver's Highland Flora
Wee Mac
Wigtown Sedric
Baldwin's Dannyquest Rebecca
Impresario's Allegro
Kirk O'The Glen's Penny Kara
Merry Tattletale
Nic-Mac's Brigadier
Snow Pixie of Ballantrae
Tam O'Leck's Jaunty John
Weaver's Highland Desmond
Wee Bonnie of the Highland
White Oaks Lover Boy
Wiloglen's Wiloughboy
Wishing Well's Winnie the Pooh
Banessa of Windy Hill
Castlemilk's Jojo John Sell
Gary's Duke of Midvale
Hi-Hopes Fair Duchess

Impresario's Jerojet Minuet
Lasara Lyn of Dannyquest
Lo-Mar's White Pebble
McTwiddle's Silver Knight
Merryhart Caper
Reanda Miss Muffet
Royal Tartan MacBrodie
Thornemore Cottage View
Wyndergael Garner
Wyndergael Sir Burton
Alpingay Eloquence
Azureglaen Skirlin' Lassie
Berwin's Dunndee Macduff
Blakely's Mace
Happymac's White Lightning
Kar Ric's Whiskey
Loch Ness Mactavish
Whitebriar Jonoke
Winsom Bridget
Checkbar Tamara Nyree
Famecheck Pilot
Flogan Forecast
Heathermoor's Dumfrie Ayr
Laird Brig-A-Doon MacDuff
Weaver's Highland Carefree
Winde Mere Pride of the Rouge

1972

Alpine's Highland Bobby
Fraley's Super Sport
Heatherscott Hellzapoppin
Merryhart Aspen Able
Pillerton Peterkin
Wiloglen's Marked Lady
Woodlawn's Desert Song
Carus Keith
Castledoon's Buffy Tarpon
Goodtime Georgie Girl
Hall's Dandi White Lass
Merryhart Chatterbox
Ollieann's Pebbles
Reanda Byline Pisces
Wiloglen's Wiloughbest

Brookline's Brandy Dune
Carus Betsy
Carus Dan D Diplomat
Dalmuir of Ranrou
Donnybrook's Douglas II
Duke Dickens of Brookline
Happymac's Tinkerbell
Lucky Lady Bug Doon MacDuff
Nato's Tuff Stuff of Wiloughby
Scotch Mist Swizzle Miss
Scotch Mist Twister Mister
Weaver's Highland Wee Mon
Willaura's Cinderella
Wishing Well's Star of Dew West
Wishing Well's Ulster Patrick
Wyndergael White Ginger
Aberdeen Jonas Mudge
Bold Charger of Ballantrae
Fairelm New Edition
Fiesty Frosty Good Girl
Happymac's Twinkle Toes
Kar Ric's Talk of the Town
Mac Wynn O' The Ridge
Royal Tartan Bonnie Brae
Winsom Mischiefmaker
Woodlawn's Debutante
Dew West Sparkling Trinket
Gay Princess of Sandyknowes
Kirk O'The Glen's Cricket
Natos Shadow, CD
Sellcrest Star Gazer
Showboat's Captain Yorktown
Sno-Bilt's Top Choice
Carroll's Pedde of D and D
Flogan Firelight
Greenbriar Grenadier
Hi Hopes Sweet William
Jolen's Heritage O'Simon
Miss Misty Dune O'Danny Quest
Punch O'Peter Pan
Sedora's Dudley Do-Right
Wishing Well's Simon's Finale
Woodlawn Destiny
Flogan Fire Bright

236

Highland Mactavish
Hilltop's See More-O-Me
Jerojet's Air Hostess
Mac-Ken-Char's Friday's Child
NorWestie's Wee Piper
Wind Crest Tiger of Dew West
Acreage's Bonnie Brandy
Annadale of Bern'F
Birkfell Star Flower
De-Go Holly
Dukendorf's Dapper Dan
Laurie's Piper of the Rouge
Nor'Westie's Wee Muff
Rannoch-Dune Jody D.
Sallydean's Macgregor's Wee Rob
Sno-Bilt's Gay Sprite
Wiloglen's Star Light
Wishing Well's Ulster Coleen
Checkbar Tommy Quite Right
Crispen Sassy Lassie
Denisette Mandan of the Rouge
Elsa of Windy Hill
Flogan Frosted Lace
Keithall Pilot
Rouse's Heidi Dukendorf
Sundance of Honan
Briarwood Ballot Box
Broon's Amiable Annie
Charlain's Age of Aquarius
Coraland MacDuff of Backmuir
Donnybrook's Daveney
Hall's Dandi Gentlemen Jim
Heritage Farm Little Patriot
Kar Ric's Genie
Ken-Ho Fair Weather
Mac-A-Dac Tiny Tim
Mr. Chips of F. D. Dee, CD
Pinecross Lucy Logan
Rosyles Pacemaker
Royal Tartan Bhana Glengarry
Rudh'Re Glendenning
Snowcliff Exemplar
Weaver's Highland Berwick
Wishing Well's Har-Lin Asteroid

Wyndergael Giselle
Dancer's Eminence of the Rouge
Dew West Banner of Ballantrae
Donnybrook's Chloe
Jerojet's Drum Major
Jerojet's Encore
Mac-A-Dac Glennora's Prize
Mac-Ken-Char's Skadiddle Riddle
Whitebriar Jinkin
Alpine's Scotch Candy
Anita's Tycoon of Sampson
Famecheck Busy Body
Highlands Angus
Illenid's Pretty Pixie
Jolen's Highland Girl by Heck
Kaspar of Moriea
Mattlen's Miss Thumbelina
Mo-Ark's Mister Luv
Purston Paddy
Roseneath Fair Charmer
Sedora's Daddy O Do-Right
Tyndrum Morar
Whitebriar Johnswort

1973

Braeburn's Clint
Famecheck Hallmark
Illenid's Pretty Matilda
Merryhart Sweet Pea
Weaver's Cee Kay Marker
White Oaks Serena The Witch
Barr's P. Penelope
Donnybrook's Rachel
Dukendorf's Big Bertha
Flogan Fall N Star
Kennelot's Bright Lad
Kincardine Centurion
Lee's Charley Bearfoot
Merryhart Happy Hobo
Rannoch-Dune Dixie
Toyoko's Yuki
Ulster Patrick's Towsie Boy
Villaview's Jiminy Cricket

237

Von Der Hellem's Scalawag
Wishing Well's Phoebe Go Litely
Birchwood's Biz O'The Ridge
Glen Shar Tia Maria
Sir Jolly Highlander
Sno-Bilt's Jill of Ballantrae
Sno-Bilt's Mighty McDuff
Weaver's Highland Rob Roy
Woodlawn's Halfpence
Kar Ric's Very Merry
Win-K's Cutty Sark
Baldwin's Four Leaf Clover
Briarwood Blockbuster
Drambuie
Jaunty MacFergus
Skaket's Lolly Pop
Toby Leigh of Thistledown
Wind Crest Super T
Wychworth Wedding March
Amy O'Tara
Dana of Windy Hill
De-Go Kiltie McLeod
Heritage Highland Heather
Hi-Hope's Chivelston Prince
Impressario's Symphony
Lochinmar Laird of Nic-Mac
Low Road's Bayou Bet O'Peter Pan
McCallum's Beau Brumble
Poppet O'Peter Pan
Purston Pitter Patter
Rannoch-Dune Delia
Buffy's Bluefish
Covintree's Glendower
Donyale of Tara Mar
Greenbriar's Binker
Hi-Hope's Fair Princess
Lo-Mar's Jewel of Eastbury
Love's Scotch and Soda
Pin-Up of Pillerton
Re-Alm's Lamplighter
Scottish Crofter
Diggory Venn of Trossachs
Kennelot's Lochinmar Lancer
Little Miss Muffin II

Lochglen Christmas Bonus
Sir Maxwell Franklin
Whitebriar Jeymin
Wigtown Zippo
Wyndergael Itsabett
Gaelcanna Canis Major
Janjac's Little Rascal
Kar Ric's Ability Again
Lochglen Christmas Bonus
Lochglen Comet
Lo-Mar's Hot Spur
London's Duffy Mac Duf
Merryhart Politician
Nic-Macs Dancing Dan
Nic-Macs Happy Talk
Wigtown Happiness Is
Wind Crest J.J. of Ballantrae
Windy Dawn Honan
Bauder's Lady Dawn
Biljonblue's Billy the Kid
Cricket O'Scots Pine
Dukendorf Debutante
Dukendorf's Hud
Glenhorm's Prince Charles
Halo's Oliver Esquire
Prosswicks Piper
Purston Polly Perkins
Windrush Wollaston
Wishing Well's Broken Drum
Famecheck Domino
Mac-Ken-Char's Heather
Rannoch-Dune Douglas
Sparrowood's Windemere Rye
Tyndrum Shuna
Wicken Calaman
Baldwin Miss Jennifer
Bonnie Brier Oliver Twofoote
Brytwood's F'Goodness Sake
Fluer of Windy Hill
Heathermoor's Hello Dolly
Nor'Westie's Able Dancer
Prosswick's Pickwick
Prosswick's Pandora
Sirius Woollawn Troll

Storybook Highwayman
Taradink Lord Dunsinane
Tasman Tarquin
Windrush Woodlark

1974

Braidholme White Tornado of Binate
Briarpatch Raggamuffin
Lutsko's Tuf Luck
White Oaks Cosmetic Storm
Briarwood Blossom
Covintree's Mystery Girl
Fitzgerald of Winsom
Flogan First Edition
Klintilloch Gin Fizz
Painted Ivory of Dorhill
Windrush Warden
Finearte Dove's Beau
Mistimont Bold Venture
Purston Pritty Pru
Whitebriar Jenise
Woodlawn's Impression
Buffy's Barracuda
Hilltop's Pickadilly
Kristajen Crackerjack
Woodlawn's Jeremy
Brookline's Wee Heather
Dennis' Dancing Dolly
Ejam's Laura of Castle Doon
Glenerin Country Cobbler
McDuff's Barney O'Simon
Scootch O'The Ridge
Sir Sundaywood Doon MacDuff
Win-K's Annie Get Your Gun
Wishing Well's Gift O'Heritage
Augustus of Flowerdale
Braeburn's Free Spirit
Donnybrook's Daniel
Flogan Fall Fire
Mistimont Snow Flurry
Ra-Den's Wee Tartan Lad
Villaview's Impressario Jamie
Birkfell Soda and Splash

Impressario's Gran Dau Thistle
Ken-Ho April Showers
Lonsdale Moonbeam
Mac-Ken-Chars Mandy Melority
Clarkcrest Colstice Carrara
Lochglen Middi-Poo
Miss Tilloch of Arlwyn
Sea Charmer of Sursumcorda
Sioux Dynamite of Halo
Snow-Bilt's Winning Streak
Wigtown Matthew
Arnholme Dove
Bluemarc's Heather
Charlain's Dawn of Aquarius
D and D's Dingies Replica
Dukendorf's Buffy
Fairbairn Lucky Star
Ken-Mar's Kelli Scot of Scotia
Lo-Mar's General Principles
Ra-Den's Helzapoppin
Skaket's Chunkies
Snowbank's Proud Poltergeist
Westwick's Wallflower
Whitebanner's Jamie
Whytehaven's De Go Headliner
Anita's Dolly of Sampson
Ardenrun Andsome of Purston
Baldwin's Bit of Honey
Birkfell Shepherd's Plaid
Buddy O'The Ridge
Carus Limelite
Flogan Fabulous Flame
Gaywyn Kara
Lucky Four Chops Hooey
Mistimont Rogue O'Castledoon
Poppea's Highland Prince
Prosswicks Perseus
Biljon's Mistymorn
Birkfell Shepherd's Pipe
Dannyquest Lucifer II
Dunemoor's Governess
Halo's First Leutenant
Kar-Ric's Faraway Fame
Lonsdale Damask

Warbonnet's Defiance
Ajax of Elsinore
Anita's Sparkle of Sampson
Braeburn's Elton's Boy
Carousel's Concert Master
Castledoon Penny Precocious
Craggencroft Impressario
Famecheck Consort
Flogan Full Fashion
Impressario's Granda Heather
Kar-Ric's Jenny Jump up
Lo Mar's Sand Piper
Merryhart Sound Off
Natos Willa
Patchwood's Gregory Griggs
Rodin's Bagpipe of D and D
Ross Hill Brigadoon
Sir Alexander McKenzie
Thayer Bro's High-Jinx Hamish
Warbonnet's Wolsey
Whitebriar Janie
Windrush The Bug of Stardust

1975

Commander of Tintibar
Happy Hill's Lucky Charm
Illusion's Sir Gaylord Scott
McCallum's Chitty Bang Bang
Reanda Wicken O'Riagain
Watts My Line
Woodlawn's Heavens To Betsy
Byline Bright Idea
Briarcliff Mornin Starshine
Reanda It's Me
Sandoone Lady Bug
Tyndrum Moidart
Jerojet's Dandi Morag
Jerojet's Memory
Kilty of Arcadia
Kincardine Kate of Brixton
Lee's Snappy Tom of Clardon
London's Bach Mai
Rogue Haven Rose

Rosemore Luvvy of Ballantrae
Sellcrest Ginger
Tiffany's Bandit O'Ballantrae
Warbonnets Orion
Weaver's Sean Cordelia
Dannycrest Short Fuse
Flogan February Snow
Highland MacSimon's Moonbeam
Highstile Pickwick
Low Road's Bobby Bruce
Nic Macs Impressario
Roughy O'Riagain
Sno-Bilt's Kiss Me Kate
Cybrook's Precious Prima Dona
Mac-Ken-Char's Johnny Ocean
Millburn Meddler
Nor'Westie's Wee Roderick
Nor'Westie's Wee Rowdy
Pedlar's Terra Doone
Rudh'Re Cantie Peigi
Serendipity Splash
Takin of Dorhill
Whytehaven's Wedgwood
Winsom Fancy Nancy
Arlwyn Greta
Bijonblue's Ali Baba
Briarcliff Benchmark
Famecheck Silver Space Man
Har-Tis Wigtown Sashay
Mac-Ken-Char's James Bonheath
Merryhart Honest John
Merryhart Sashay
Sedora's Korki Do-Right
Whyte Imp's Allegro
Birkfell Sweet and Lovely
Cedarfell Morning Parody
Dawnwind Birkfell
Dunemoor Fluffernutter
Halo's Jiminy Cricket
Hecker's Hercules by Heck
Highland Macchevious
Illusion's Sir Robin Lochsley
Kennelot's Leapin' Lizzie
Kirk O'The Glen Toby

240

Lonsdale Buckram
Marilda's Frosty Munchkin
Merryhart Jumpin' Jack
Rose Marie's Mean Mary Jean
Roseneath Candy Man
Sioux Nitro-Glycerine
Sir Slippet's Thegn, CD
Teaka's Crystal Clear
Thornecorft Pollyanna
Weaver's Highland Deena, CD
Wicken Greenbriar Eagan
Briarpatch Shaunassy
Killikranky Hi Jinx
Nor'Westie's Wee Charger
Prosswick's Promise
Renlim Refrain
Tamlane's Wee Frazier
Woodlawn's Rendition
Benincasa's White Sunshine
Birkfell Shepherd Dance
Flogan Fall Days
Greenbriar Galaxy
Halo's Magic Angel
Heather of Arlwyn
Mac-Ken-Char's Mariposa
Rannoch-Dune Dupli Kate
Roseneath Maxwell Smart
Skaket's WinniPooh
Whitebriar Jamieson
Whitebriar Jervish
Whytehaven's Wildflower
Aberdeen's Barnaby Rudge
BJ's Sir Ballot
Castlemilk's Dennmarr
Checkbar Peg-O-Ramsay
Elmac's Merrie Andrew
Finearte Dove's Pearl
Fulton's Frosty Holly
Happymac's Li'l Mischief Maker
Heatherscott Humdinger
Kingmont Bar-Dan Dannie Boy
Nic-Mac's Mica
Watts His Name
Windmere Rabbie O'Riagain

Winsom Sparkle Plenty
Wyndergael Big Dandy
BJ's Sir Becket
Bonny Brier Sunny Dae-Girl
Clyde of Creag Meagaidh
Glengidge Precocious
Hillary of Windy Hill
Mark's Lad of Halo
Nor'Westie's Wee Jessie
Ronell's Tammy T
Whitebriar Jixmas
Woodlawn's Country Squire
Woodlawn's Rambling Rose

1976

Charlain's Deacon
Kennelot's Legal Larceny
Kincardine Cavalier
Reanda Desert Rat
Theodorabliz of Donnrich
Trethmore Twopence-Off
BJ's Baby Grand
Bonnie Prince Charlie XIII
Kingmont's Timmy O' Mac-Ken-Char
Jim O' Jen's Man Man
Lonsdale Dimity
Natos Snowflake
Neal's Wishing Star
Nor-Westie's Wee Fancy
Rushpark Rebecca
Sedora's Austin McClullen
Solstice's Lotta Hooey
Bracken's Beau Jester
Illusion's Judy's Pride
J-Mac's Toughman
Ken-Ho Big Thunder
Lady Charlotte of Cameron
Lo-Mar's Michael II
Roseneath Great Scot
Sarabliz of Donnrich
Woodlawn's Minute Man
Laird Doon MacDuff of Lyon
Little Kilt's Perky Piper

Nic-Mac's Lady of Happy Hill
Noah
Rannoch Dune Drummer II
Royalkirk's Ramblin Rosie
Byline Highland Quince
Callagrange Lord Chaucer
Cybrook's April Holly
Merryhart Love Child
Purston Predictable
Baldwin's Talisman Terri
Bonnie Brier Barbet
Jaycee's Joyful Jason
Ji-Ro's Free Spirit
Patriot of Prosswick
Robinswood Bobbie Shatoe
Bayou Glen's Reverend Mike
Biljonblue's Friar Tuck
Edinboro's Flim Flam Man
Jentre's Frostpoint
Loch Lomond Sea Mist
Maggie McGinnes
Nor'Westie's Wee Pixie
Purston Peacemaker
Sedora's Daisy Doll
Sir Chumley of Twin View
Snowbank Same Ol' Shenanigan
Whitebriar Jofane
Bonnie Brier Lionel Two Foote
Charlain's Holly-Go-Love-Leah
Dawnwind Highlander's Mac
Happy Hill's Shannon
Happy Hill's White Mist
Pillerton Pip
Tiffany's Mr. Mark

Whitebriar Jaspuck
Whytehaven's Windsong
Woodlawn's Legacy
Aspen's MacAuthur
Jul-Don-Skidmore of the Kilts
Lo-Mar's Parader
Pennysworth O'Peter Pan
Pillerton Priceless
Tav-A-Mac's Tartan Tumblebug
Woodlawn's Dividend
Arcadia's Avalanche
Biljonblue's Butch Cassidy
Briarcliff Blackjack
Donnybrook's Nickel's Worth
Lee's Happy Holli
Maclyn's Sailor Boy
Sedora's McDuff Doll Baby
Skaket's Lady MacDuff
Tiddle Dee Winks
Windward Paddy Waggin'
Belvar's Theodore J. Bear
BJ's Sir Brevit
Bonnybrook Aurora
Bonnycastle Special Event
Briarpatch Brechin
Charlain's Sign of Aquarius
D and D's Aim-Us of Melrose
Kenarth Lowrie
Kirk O the Glen's Toorie M' Weyin
Linwood's Winsome Fanny
Mauradoon's Silver Jubilee
Meddlesome Mollye T. Sq
Suncrest Bam of Glendonyn
Whytehaven's Wedding Belle

(Unless otherwise noted all dogs are holders of the C.D. degree.)

1970

Ch. Crest O'Lake Mighty Mac
Candida of Vallette
Lady Tam O'Shanter II
Sir Whytdale Blue Banner
Sno-Bilt's Lord Jim
Arlwyn Ginn Phizz
Mar'Grin's Beag Caill Leannan
Tamoshanter VII
King Whitehall
Mar'Grin's Hoot Mon
Ka-Le's Heather Hildegard
Smokey McDew
Weaver's Highland Fidelia
Barr's P. Pringle, C.D.X.
Vimy Ridge Catriona, C.D.X., T.D.
Bit of Paradise Hi Soo

1971

May's Ruffled Lassie
Ch. Dew West Pep Si Mac Aroon
Natos Shadow
Reed's McDuff, C.D.X.
Alfie, C.D.X.
Loch Lomond's Popcorn
Tacksman Jeannie
Wee Wooer's Wishen-U-Well
Wilkin's Mister Charles
Ch. Wee White Wooer, C.D.X.
Kelly's Duncan of Villaview
Nato's Wiloglen Spark O'Mark
Sno-Bilt's Ragadee Andy
Tamoshanter VII, C.D.X.
Bev-Vic's Little Miss Fizzle

1972

Happy Harvey of Hawthorn
Mr. Chips of F. D. Dee
Dunvegan Bonnie Heather
Heather Charlain MacTavish
William Wesley MacTavish

Craggencroft Simply Simon
Davenport's Jigger of Scotch
Rosent's Sure Sally
Ch. Snow Pixie of Ballantrae
Arlwyn Ginn's Tonic
Castledoon's Petersham
McTwiddles Little Ben Gunn
Tui Mei Lon
Weaver's Highland Design
Cornell's Sir Fuzzer McDuff
Little Sir Echo II
Nic-Macs Mr. Chips O'Nine Tree
Craggencroft Simply Simon, C.D.X.
Happy Harvey of Hawthorn, C.D.X.
El-Da Tamara of Ardoon
White Oaks Great Flegale
Hermit's Candice Jane
Natos Wiloglen Sparl O-Mark, C.D.X.
Barr's P. Pringle, U.D.
Acreages Parader
Ch. Barr's P. Phoebe
Ka-Le's Heather Hildegard, C.D.X.
Graham's Little Lu-Lu

1973

Kar Ric's Jolly Jester
Roseneath Holly of Lindum
Davenport's Jigger of Scotch, C.D.X.
Highland Wicket
Hillary's Dixie Belle
Argyle Princess
Beaver McBeke
Brigadoon's Image of Meg
Ch. Goodtime Georgie Girl
Ch. Loch Ness Mactavish
Miss Mae's Muffett
Mr. McWiffit
Ch. Sedora's Dudley Do-Right
Sir Adam of Glengarry
Ch. Crest-O-Lake Mighty Mac, C.D.X.
Katharine MacFie of Kennelot
Braeburn's Colin MacAndrew
Sir Slippet's Thegn

Aindreas Glendonyn MacDune
Ch. Craggencroft Cuddihy, C.D.X.
Kar Ric's Jolly Jester, C.D.X.
Coles Misty Frost
D and D's English Ragamuffin
Lord Territon
Sientese De Recha
Breezy of Cooley
Sandy's Frosty Snowgirl
Sir Boss MacCloud
Wee Honey Ball
Craggencroft Jillikyns Lass
Ka-Le's Kilted Karma

1974

Craggencroft Cocklarachy
Glencoe's Brandywine
White Acres Gae Heather
Barnabas of Birch
Ferguson of Windy Hill
JJ's Whiskey Snow Drift
Ch. Rannoch-Dune Diavolo
Sellcrest Miss Ninetree
Alfie III, U.D.
Davenport's Jigger of Scotch, U.D.
Ch. Goodtime Georgie Girl, C.D.X.
Beth's Windsong
White Heather of Douglas
Cornell's Tiny Snowflake
Sioux Chief Tecumseh
Weaver's Highland Deena
Braeburn's Colin MacAndrew, C.D.X.
Amanda of Starhaven
Bonnie Brier Misty Morning
Klintilloch Chivas Regal
Tiffany's Frosty Lady
Evan O'Scots Pine
Smokey McDew, C.D.X.
Bonnie Brier Molly
Our Presumptuous Lady Tuck
Gayblade Tish
Robbie McTavish Linklater
Skyhills Thunder
Windermere of Rosewood

1975

Ch. Lochinmar Laird of Nic-Mac
Little Sir Echo, C.D.X.
Amstel of Starhaven
Miss Tina
Our Little Bandit
Kelly's Duncan of Villaview, C.D.X.
Happymac's Bickett of MacDuff
Lady Bonnie Sue McTavish
Sir Prescott of Shelburne
Wee Heather Westie
Lucky Four Stewart O'Riagain
Charlotte's Sugar and Cream
Argyle Princess
Miss Mae Muffet
Doug's Delightful Daisy, U.D.
Halo's Whippersnapper
Ch. Skaket's Chunkies
Wee Honey Hall, C.D.X.
Ch. Bonnie Brier Oliver Twofoote
Ch. Loch Crest Lady Caroline
Lord Territon, C.D.X.
MacDuff of Can-Crest
Cole's Rob Roy
Pip's Chuckles of the Rouge
Glenhaven's Gabrielle

1976

Francisco's Bonnie Wee Joshua
Timothy Tort Kelsey
White Streaker
Duchess Joanne
Tav-A-Mac's Muff 'N' Tuff
Maggart's Little Rumpus
Tasha Lynn Fleming
Teloca Scooter of Quite Right
Weaver's Highland Annabelle
Beth's Trusty Soul
Lady Sassafras Wine
Rannoch-Dune Michie Banjo
Klintilloch Katie Sunshine
Meaghan's O'Riagain
Sweeney's Scotch Rocket

244

Castlemilk's Withywindle
Lady Deedee O'Ninetree
Skaket's Little Bip
Ch. Kilty of Arcadia
Winnie Blackburn
High Pockets Casey
Prosswick's Phantom
Arcadia's Avalanche
Bonnie Brier Misty Morning, C.D.X.
Effrem of Windy Hill

Boettcher's Jack Frost
Glenbrier Prancing Piper
Lynn's Scotty MacTavish
Meikle MacTay
Russtine's Willow Creek Trudy
Sno-Bilt's Megs of Brixham
Ch. Villaview's Jiminy Cricket
Ch. Watts His Name
Beth's Windsong, C.D.X.

Westies doing what they were bred for. The scene is a working terrier trial as this energetic pack is off to locate the game. Working trials for terrier breeds are a recent development and encourage fanciers of Westies and all earth-going terriers to remain mindful of their breeds' admirable, natural heritage.

Trends and Observations

During recent years, the numerical position of the West Highlander has improved dramatically. It has progressed from a little-known and seldom seen breed in the thirties and forties to one of the most popular strains in the Terrier group. Such a change in position heralds a corresponding rise in the number of fanciers who support the breed. The majority of this group, while long on enthusiasm, is very short of useful knowledge or breed background. These same newcomers, because of their relative numbers often establish trends which are frequently looked upon as the rule, rather than the exception. This unfortunate situation will be surveyed with respect to presentation in the paragraphs to follow.

To forestall further inroads of this nature let me say that the charm of the West Highland White Terrier is intensified by proper "tidying up." This does not mean *extreme* trimming. The Westie is a natural breed, this is one of the reasons why so many have been drawn to it. In this day of heavily trimmed breeds such as the Poodle, it is refreshing to find a breed that does not require extreme trimming to look its best. In fact, it has been said and very properly, that a well-presented Westie should appear untrimmed while offering a neat and immaculate

246

overall image. This is surely true, and it leaves little room for the heavily trimmed specimens sometimes seen in the rings. Furthermore, many of these have never had a plucking knife used on them, only scissors, razors and clippers as is evident to any experienced person. None of these last three mentioned tools is required in the tidying up of a Westie. All can be used to advantage and offer shortcuts over the slower and more desirable method of plucking and when properly applied do not leave evidence of use. However, none can improve nor even maintain correct coat texture.

Trimming requires a great deal of patience and more than a modicum of knowledge. The art cannot be learned overnight but requires study and practice before a novice can hope to present a properly trimmed dog. This does not mean that dogs conditioned through the early efforts of an amateur cannot be shown since in many cases they can win over a better presented animal because they are a better specimen. It does mean, however, that expert trimming presents a dog better and offers a better chance of winning when the competition is close.

The tendency to remove all the hair around the face, that which we refer to as "a frame" is deplored by all true supporters of the breed. Its removal ruins the charm of the breed and deprives the dog of its very characteristic outlook.

Similarly, too much ruff is equally poor practice. Westies are sometimes seen with a large, symmetrically scissored frame or ruff that resembles a "sun-burst" in both size and shape. This over-balances the entire dog and ruins expression while detracting from type. The ruff should be offered in moderate terms, not too much nor too little. It should be in balance with the remainder of the animal so that the head does not detract from the total picture. Another failing seen too often today is the stripping off of all neck hair so that the head with its ruff appears completely out of balance with the remainder of the animal, much like "an apple on a stick." The neck should have a generous covering of hair. This may be well blended into both the head and the body by proper trimming so that the final product does not seem artificial and

247

out-of-balance. These nuances in trimming are what separates the truly skillful craftsman from most others and always offer substantial benefits to the dog that is properly trimmed without exaggeration.

A Westie should never be artificially presented which always results from over-trimming. Some of this tendency can also be laid at the feet of overly zealous professional handlers who are becoming more in evidence as the breed numbers increase. The professional, of all people, should learn the proper way to present the breed *before* accepting fees for trimming and showing other people's dogs. That many handlers have mastered the art of setting down the Highlander is evident from the myriad of illustrations in this book showing professionals with their well put-down charges.

Three other points that have not before been emphasized in the chapter on trimming, and which bear additional comment, concern eyes, ears and neck line. Eyes are the very soul of the breed. Westie eyes are not beady, little eyes and, in spite of the Standard, can quite properly be dark hazel rather than black. In fact, few have black eyes. In any event, since the eyes are the main source of expression they should of necessity be visible. Too much hair around the eyes with overly long drooping eyebrows hide the eyes and thus cause loss of expression. In trimming the head, see to it that the eyes are visible; they are a basic breed characteristic. This can best be accomplished by separating the eyebrows by careful trimming and removing some hair at the stop adjacent to the eyes.

Ears too require attention in trimming. Quite frequently dogs are seen in which the ears have been cleaned off to the base which certainly makes the ears appear overly large and in some cases mule-like. Ears should be fairly clean from the tips about half-way down; thereafter, they should have plenty of hair which blends into the longer hair of the head and frame. This improves the expression and goes a long way towards creating the illusion that the ears are smaller and sometimes better set than perhaps they are.

The neck line should be emphasized without removing all of the hair from the top of the neck. By carrying good length of coat on the top of the neck and blending it properly into the body at the withers it is possible to create the illusion of a short back and well-laid-back shoulders even when a dog does not excel in these points. If the dog does have good shoulders this mode of trimming still further improves his general appearance. A heavily trimmed neck does not blend into the body and gives the impression of a short neck and straight shoulders even when these faults do not exist.

Another comment concerns coats. The Standard *requires* that a proper Westie coat should be about two inches in length. Many are being shown today with coats not over one inch in length on the body. This length may be easier to care for but it robs the dog of many of its attributes. A proper length of top coat tends to raise the dog off the ground, appearance-wise, and removes the impression that the dog is too short on leg. This is particularly true when the exhibitor leaves a full length of skirt that barely clears the ground. A Westie *should* be up on the leg, it should not be very close to the ground and a short-legged Highlander is not the proper type. Yet the very mode of trimming practiced by many, the absence of proper length of coat, accentuates the fault. Show your dogs with two inches of top coat; they will look better and will more nearly exemplify the breed desideratum.

These few comments on trimming, while critical in tone, are meant to be helpful. Too many persons pursue the wrong course only because they do not have the proper information. It is hoped that these remarks coupled with the fuller dissertation on the entire subject in the chapter on trimming will help rectify the situation.

Observation of many dogs at the top shows in both England and the United States starting during the middle sixties substantiates the author's beliefs that there is a tendency within the breed to lose size. Dogs, in many instances, are no larger than the average bitch. This trend, if allowed to continue, will injure the breed since size is an important adjunct to winning in inter-breed competition. It is seldom that a good little dog does well in the groups and this applies to all breeds. The same dog may win well in the breed but is seldom first in inter-breed competition. Further, dogs that are up to size appear more masculine and, experience has demonstrated, make better sires. This observation applies to all breeds as well since it is seldom that a small dog becomes a great stud force.

Fortunately, most of the big winners in the United States still have sufficient size but many dogs gaining less acclaim are more on the order of a bitch than a dog. If the trend is not stopped, the breed will suffer ultimately. I am at a loss to know why this is happening and can only hazard a guess that it comes from too much close breeding. It has been my experience, that close breeding through a number of generations causes loss of size. If this is the case, a few out-cross breedings or at least some more distant breeding may help the situation.

One last comment concerns present day heads. The Standard states unequivocally that the "muzzle should be slightly shorter than the skull" and that the skull "should be fairly broad—and not too long." It further states under "faults"—"muzzle longer than skull" and skulls that are "too long or too narrow." These are very explicit definitions, yet in the ring today we are seeing many abortive heads, long skulls, and even longer forefaces. This type of head destroys the characteristic expression of the Highlander and gives it a hard expression. It is hoped that breeders will get down to basics and stop breeding from animals with these faults. Now is the time to stop the trend.

Thus ends this book on the Highlander. May it help each of you to better appreciate the breed for show, for breeding and as companions that have no equal, for as Dr. Gordon Stables wrote almost a century ago:

The Terrier From The North

Losh' Bogie man haud off your han';
  Nor thrash me black and blue.
Frae fools and foes I seek nae praise,
  But frien's should aye be true.

Nae silky-haired admirer I
  O'Bradford Toys, Strathbogie;
Sich thoughts, I'm sure cam' in your head,
  While dribblin' o'er the cogie.

I ken the Terrier o'the North,
  I ken the towsy tyke—
Ye'll search frae Tweed to Sussex' shore,
  But never find his like.

For pluck and pith and jaws and teeth,
  And hair like heather cowes,
Wi' body lang and low and strang,
  At hame in cairns or knowes.

He'll face a foumart, draw a brock,
  Kill rats and whitteritts by the score,
He'll bang tod-Lowrie frae his hole,
  Or slay him at his door.

He'll range for days and ne'er be tired,
  O'er mountain, moor, and fell;
Fair play, I'll back the brave wee chap
  To fecht the de'il himsel'.

And yet beneath his rugged coat
  A heart beats warm and true.
He'll help to herd the sheep and kye,
  And mind the lammies too.

Then see him at the ingle side,
  Wi' bairnies roond him laughin'.
Was ever dog sae pleased as he,
  Sae fond o'fun and daffin'?

But gie's your hand, Strathbogie man'
  Guid faith' we maunna sever.
Then 'Here's to Scotia's best o'dogs,
  Our towsy tyke for ever!' ".

(The Live Stock Journal, Jan. 31st)
By Dr. Gordon Stables, 1879

Foumart—A Polecat
Brock—A Badger
Whitteritts—A Weasel
Tod—A Fox

BIOLOGICAL FACTS AND DATA

Vital Signs for Adult Dogs Under Generally Normal Conditions

Normal Temperature taken rectally: 101.5°–102°F

Normal pulse rate: 80 to about 120 per minute

Normal respiration: 10 to 30 per minute

Age of Maturity and Mating Facts

Sexual maturity in dogs occurs at from about seven to nine months of age but this may vary. However, the American Kennel Club will not register puppies by a sire less than seven months old at time of mating.

Bitches normally have their first Oestrous cycle (period of heat) at about nine months of age although it may come earlier or later. The American Kennel Club will not register puppies born out of a bitch less than eight months old at the time of mating.

The Oestrous cycle lasts about three weeks. The most appropriate time for planned mating is after the discharge has become generally colorless, between ten to fourteen days. A bitch will come in season normally two times each year at six month intervals.

The period of gestation for puppies is normally 63 days from the breeding date. This may vary slightly and puppies are frequently whelped at from four days early to one or two days late.

Puppy Facts

Eyes open between nine and twelve days from whelping date.

Weaning should begin at from five to six weeks of age, depending upon the strength of the puppies and the extent of teething.

Teething begins at from four to five weeks of age, while permanent incisors with the shedding of milk teeth starts at from two to five months of age. The canine (large tusk-like dentition) and cheek teeth (Premolars and molars) come in from about four-and-a-half to seven months of age. Dogs vary one from another in all of these and the foregoing ages are approximations offered solely as a general guide.

Never dock Westie tails. Some veterinary books suggest such a procedure. *It is wrong.* Be sure your veterinarian is not mis-informed in this important particular. A Westie with a docked tail is permanently ruined for the show ring.

In any situation that appears to be abnormal, the best procedure is to consult immediately with your veterinarian. Many problems that have become serious could have been averted by following this admonition.

Bibliography

The following list of books and magazine articles is offered for those who wish to delve further into background on the West Highland White Terrier. It will also be a useful guide to fanciers who wish to assemble a comprehensive library on the breed.

Books:

THE DOGS OF SCOTLAND. D. J. Thomson Gray (Whinstone) . Dundee, 1891. This book includes a chapter on the Poltalloch Terrier and is probably the earliest reference to the breed. Exceedingly rare.

MODERN DOGS. The Terriers. Rawdon Lee. London, 1894. A general history of the Terrier breeds. Pages 253–255 include information on the Highlander together with a letter written by Col. Malcolm.

DOG SHOWS AND DOGGY PEOPLE. C. H. Lane. London, 1902, pages 100–102. References to Dr. Flaxman.

DOGS—BY WELL KNOWN AUTHORITIES. Edited by Harding Cox. London, 1906. The Terrier volume of this rare book includes a chapter on the breed written by Col. E. D. Malcolm, pages 89 through 93, Vol. 1. Also a full page colored plate of "Boidheach" by Margaret Collyer. The chapter is sometimes found as an entity. Both the book and the separate chapter are very scarce.

THE NEW BOOK OF THE DOG. Robert Leighton. London, 1907. Includes a chapter on the breed by Col. Malcolm, pages 390 through 396, Vol. 2.

THE KENNEL ENCYCLOPEDIA. J. Sidney Turner. London. 1907–11. Includes an excellent chapter on the breed by Mrs. Cameron-Head, pages 1462–1474.

OTTERS AND OTTER HUNTING. L. C. R. Cameron. London, 1908, pages 42–43.

HUTCHINSON'S DOG ENCYCLOPEDIA. Compiled by Walter Hutchinson. London, 1935. Includes a chapter (pages 1902–1919) on the breed by E. C. Ash.

OUR FRIEND THE WEST HIGHLAND. Rowland Johns. London, 1935. A small book of the popular order.

WEST HIGHLAND WHITE TERRIERS. May Pacey. London, 1963. A small book directed almost entirely to British efforts.

THE WEST HIGHLAND WHITE TERRIER. D. Mary Dennis. London, 1967. Written by the owner of the Branston Kennels, this book offers information concerning English dogs and English dog shows.

THE POPULAR CAIRN TERRIER. J. W. H. Benyon. London, 1930. Offers some interesting observations regarding the derivation of the Scottish, Cairn and West Highland White Terriers, together with pedigrees of dogs that include all three.

SCOTTISH AND WEST HIGHLAND WHITE TERRIERS. McCandlish and Powlett. Manchester, Eng. 1909. The chapter on Westies is by B. W. Powlett and will be found on pages 70–80.

THE WEST HIGHLAND WHITE TERRIER. Holland Buckley. London, 1911. The first book devoted exclusively to the breed.

THE CAIRN TERRIER. Florence M. Ross. Manchester, Eng. 1925. Contains an interesting chapter (Chap. V, pages 39–48) on the interbreeding of Cairns and Westies.

DOGS, THEIR HISTORY AND DEVELOPMENT. E. C. Ash. London, 1927. Includes a good chapter on the breed.

THE COMPLETE ILLUSTRATED WEST HIGHLAND WHITE TERRIER. Joe and Liz Cartledge. London, 1973.

During the past few years there have been several small paper-backed books published in the U.S. offering information to pet owners. These are generally available at pet shops and department stores.

Magazine Articles:

THE TERRIERS OF POLTALLOCH. Country Life (London), May 11, 1901, pages 588–590.

WEST HIGHLAND TERRIERS. Country Life (London), Aug. 14, 1909, page 242.

CAIRN TERRIERS. Country Life (London), Sept. 23, 1911, pages 454–456. This article is on Westies despite the title.

THE POLTALLOCH WHITE TERRIERS. Country Life (London), Nov. 5, 1921, pages 570–572.

THE TERRIERS OF SCOTLAND. Country Life (London), Sept. 2, 1922, pages 267–268.

WHOM GLORY CANNOT WELL FORGET. American Kennel Gazette, Nov. 1926, pages 28–32. A history of the Nishkenon Kennels.

ROSSTOR, ROLLING STONE OF DOGDOM. American Kennel Gazette, Feb. 1927, pages 9–13, 84–85. A history of the Rosstor Kennels.

BONNIE BAIRNES OF EDGERSTOUNE. American Kennel Gazette, Nov. 1931, pages 9–13, 122–124. A history of the famous Edgerstoune Kennels.

THE JOY THAT WINNING BRINGS. American Kennel Gazette, March 1931, pages 33–34.

WHY EDGERSTOUNE SUCCEEDS. American Kennel Gazette, Dec. 1934, pages 25–29, 196. Additional information concerning Edgerstoune.

WHITE EARTH DOGGES. Kennel and Bench (Canada), Sept. 1938, pages 16–17. An article by Anne Elizabeth Blochin.

DOGS AND SPORT IN SCOTLAND. American Kennel Gazette, Feb. 1939, pages 12–15. An article by Freeman Lloyd with heavy emphasis on the Westie.

THE WEST HIGHLAND WHITE TERRIER. Popular Dogs (U.S.), Sept. 1952, pages 24–25. An article by J. Neill Malcolm.

PLANS FOR THE WESTIE. Popular Dogs (U.S.), Sept. 1952, pages 25–27. An article by Dorothea Daniell-Jenkins.

255

BIBLIOGRAPHY

ALL OWNERS of pure-bred dogs will benefit themselves and their dogs by enriching their knowledge of breeds and of canine care, training, breeding, psychology and other important aspects of dog management. The following list of books covers further reading recommended by judges, veterinarians, breeders, trainers and other authorities. Books may be obtained at the finer book stores and pet shops, or through Howell Book House Inc., publishers, New York.

Breed Books

AFGHAN HOUND, Complete	Miller & Gilbert
AIREDALE, New Complete	Edwards
AKITA, Complete	Linderman & Funk
ALASKAN MALAMUTE, Complete	Riddle & Seeley
BASSET HOUND, Complete	Braun
BEAGLE, New Complete	Noted Authorities
BLOODHOUND, Complete	Brey & Reed
BORZOI, Complete	Groshans
BOXER, Complete	Denlinger
BRITTANY SPANIEL, Complete	Riddle
BULLDOG, New Complete	Hanes
BULL TERRIER, New Complete	Eberhard
CAIRN TERRIER, Complete	Marvin
CHESAPEAKE BAY RETRIEVER, Complete	Cherry
CHIHUAHUA, Complete	Noted Authorities
COCKER SPANIEL, New	Kraeuchi
COLLIE, New	Official Publication of the Collie Club of America
DACHSHUND, The New	Meistrell
DALMATIAN, The	Treen
DOBERMAN PINSCHER, New	Walker
ENGLISH SETTER, New Complete	Tuck, Howell & Graef
ENGLISH SPRINGER SPANIEL, New	Goodall & Gasow
FOX TERRIER, New Complete	Silvernail
GERMAN SHEPHERD DOG, New Complete	Bennett
GERMAN SHORTHAIRED POINTER, New	Maxwell
GOLDEN RETRIEVER, Complete	Fischer
GREAT DANE, New Complete	Noted Authorities
GREAT DANE, The—Dogdom's Apollo	Draper
GREAT PYRENEES, Complete	Strang & Giffin
IRISH SETTER, New	Thompson
IRISH WOLFHOUND, Complete	Starbuck
KEESHOND, Complete	Peterson
LABRADOR RETRIEVER, Complete	Warwick
LHASA APSO, Complete	Herbel
MINIATURE SCHNAUZER, Complete	Eskrigge
NEWFOUNDLAND, New Complete	Chern
NORWEGIAN ELKHOUND, New Complete	Wallo
OLD ENGLISH SHEEPDOG, Complete	Mandeville
PEKINGESE, Quigley Book of	Quigley
PEMBROKE WELSH CORGI, Complete	Sargent & Harper
POODLE, New Complete	Hopkins & Irick
POODLE CLIPPING AND GROOMING BOOK, Complete	Kalstone
PULI, Complete	Owen
SAMOYED, Complete	Ward
SCHIPPERKE, Official Book of	Root, Martin, Kent
SCOTTISH TERRIER, New Complete	Marvin
SHETLAND SHEEPDOG, The New	Riddle
SHIH TZU, Joy of Owning	Seranne
SHIH TZU, The (English)	Dadds
SIBERIAN HUSKY, Complete	Demidoff
TERRIERS, The Book of All	Marvin
WEST HIGHLAND WHITE TERRIER, Complete	Marvin
WHIPPET, Complete	Pegram
YORKSHIRE TERRIER, Complete	Gordon & Bennett

Breeding

ART OF BREEDING BETTER DOGS, New	Onsto
BREEDING YOUR OWN SHOW DOG	Seranr
HOW TO BREED DOGS	Whitne
HOW PUPPIES ARE BORN	Pri
INHERITANCE OF COAT COLOR IN DOGS	Lit

Care and Training

DOG OBEDIENCE, Complete Book of	Saunde
NOVICE, OPEN AND UTILITY COURSES	Saunde
DOG CARE AND TRAINING FOR BOYS AND GIRLS	Saund
DOG NUTRITION, Collins Guide to	Col
DOG TRAINING FOR KIDS	Benja
DOG TRAINING, Koehler Method of	Koe
DOG TRAINING, Step by Step Manual	Volhard & Fis
GO FIND! Training Your Dog to Track	D
GUARD DOG TRAINING, Koehler Method of	Koe
OPEN OBEDIENCE FOR RING, HOME AND FIELD, Koehler Method of	Koe
STONE GUIDE TO DOG GROOMING FOR ALL BREEDS	S
SUCCESSFUL DOG TRAINING, The Pearsall Guide to	Pea
TOY DOGS, Kalstone Guide to Grooming All	Kals
TRAINING THE RETRIEVER	Ke
TRAINING YOUR DOG TO WIN OBEDIENCE TITLES	Mc
TRAIN YOUR OWN GUN DOG, How to	Go
UTILITY DOG TRAINING, Koehler Method of	Ko
VETERINARY HANDBOOK, Dog Owner's Home	Carlson &

General

CANINE TERMINOLOGY	
COMPLETE DOG BOOK, The	Official Publica American Kenne
DOG IN ACTION, The	
DOG BEHAVIOR, New Knowledge of	Pfaffen
DOG JUDGE'S HANDBOOK	
DOG JUDGING, Nicholas Guide to	Ni
DOG PEOPLE ARE CRAZY	
DOG PSYCHOLOGY	W
DOGSTEPS, Illustrated Gait at a Glance	
DOG TRICKS	Haggerty & Be
ENCYCLOPEDIA OF DOGS, International	Dangerfield, Howell &
FROM RICHES TO BITCHES	S
IN STITCHES OVER BITCHES	S
JUNIOR SHOWMANSHIP HANDBOOK	Brown &
MY TIMES WITH DOGS	F
OUR PUPPY'S BABY BOOK (blue or pink)	
SUCCESSFUL DOG SHOWING, Forsyth Guide to	
TRIM, GROOM AND SHOW YOUR DOG, How to	S
WHY DOES YOUR DOG DO THAT?	B
WILD DOGS in Life and Legend	
WORLD OF SLED DOGS, From Siberia to Sport	C